CLOUD INFRASTRUCTURE FOR GENERATIVE AI

A Beginners guide to understand cloud Infrastructure for gen AI

Sumit Potdar

Sumit Potdar
Visit my website at www.sumitpotdar.com

Printed in the United States of America

First Printing: Dec 2024
House Of Tech Books

ISBN-979-8-3029193-7-3

CONTENTS

Purpose and Scope of the Book

Introduction

Understand purpose and scope of the book

The rapidly evolving landscape of artificial intelligence (AI) and cloud computing has revolutionized various industries and opened up new possibilities. This book, Cloud Infrastructure for Generative AI: Building the Future of Intelligent Systems, aims to provide a comprehensive guide for leveraging cloud infrastructure to enhance and deploy generative AI applications. It serves as a practical handbook for AI practitioners, cloud engineers, and data scientists who are eager to explore the intersection of these cutting-edge technologies.

Purpose of the Book

The primary purpose of this book is to bridge the knowledge gap between generative AI and cloud infrastructure. While numerous resources focus individually on AI algorithms and cloud computing, there is a lack of integrated material that combines both areas. This book seeks to fulfill this gap by offering detailed insights, practical guidelines, and real-world examples that showcase how cloud infrastructure can be effectively utilized to develop, train, deploy, and scale generative AI models.

Objectives

The objectives of this book are manifold:

- **Educational Insight:** To provide a thorough understanding of generative AI and cloud computing fundamentals, ensuring readers grasp the essential concepts and technologies.
- **Practical Application:** To offer step-by-step guidance on setting up cloud environments, managing data, training AI models, and deploying solutions in the cloud.
- **Industry Relevance:** To present case studies and real-world applications, demonstrating the practical implications and benefits of integrating generative AI with cloud infrastructure.
- **Scalability and Optimization:** To explore strategies for optimizing performance, managing costs, and ensuring scalability and reliability of AI systems in the cloud.
- **Security and Compliance:** To address the critical aspects of security, privacy, and compliance, providing best practices for safeguarding AI projects in the cloud.

Target Audience

This book is intended for a diverse audience, including:

- **AI Practitioners and Data Scientists**: Professionals working on AI projects who seek to leverage cloud infrastructure to enhance their generative AI applications.
- **Cloud Engineers and Architects:** Individuals responsible for designing and managing cloud environments who want to understand the specific requirements and challenges of AI workloads.
- **Technical Managers and Decision Makers:** Leaders in technology and business who need to make informed decisions about adopting and integrating cloud-based AI solutions.
- **Students and Researchers**: Aspiring AI professionals and academic researchers looking to deepen their knowledge of cloud infrastructure and its application in generative AI.

Scope of the Book

The scope of this book encompasses the following key areas:

- **Introduction to Cloud Computing and Generative AI:** Laying the foundation with basic concepts and an overview of both fields.
- **Setting Up Cloud Environments:** Detailed instructions on provisioning and configuring compute resources, storage solutions, and networking for AI workloads.

- **Data Management and Processing:** Techniques for data ingestion, preprocessing, and storage, tailored to the needs of generative AI.
- **Training and Deployment of AI Models:** Best practices for training AI models on cloud infrastructure, including distributed training, model deployment, and serving.
- **Scalability and Performance:** Strategies for scaling AI workloads, optimizing performance, and ensuring high availability and reliability.
- **Security and Compliance:** Guidelines for maintaining security, privacy, and regulatory compliance in cloud-based AI projects.
- **Cost Management:** Insights into managing and optimizing costs associated with cloud infrastructure for AI.
- **Case Studies and Applications:** Real-world examples and success stories that illustrate the practical application of generative AI in the cloud.
- **Future Directions and Innovations:** Exploring emerging trends, technologies, and future opportunities in the realm of cloud infrastructure for generative AI.

CHAPTER 1
Introduction to Generative AI

This Chapter is an overview of Generative AI

Generative AI represents a groundbreaking advancement in the field of artificial intelligence, enabling machines to create new content, ideas, and solutions that were previously thought to be the exclusive domain of human creativity. This chapter provides an overview of generative AI, its applications, and its significance in today's technological landscape.

What is Generative AI?

Generative AI refers to a class of artificial intelligence models designed to generate new data that resembles a given dataset. Unlike traditional AI models that focus on classification or prediction, generative AI models create new content, such as text, images, music, and even entire virtual environments. These models learn the underlying patterns and structures of the input data and use this knowledge to produce novel outputs.

Key Concepts and Techniques

- **Generative Adversarial Networks (GANs):** GANs consist of two neural networks, a generator and a discriminator, that work together in a competitive setting. The generator creates new data, while the discriminator evaluates its authenticity. Through this adversarial process, GANs can produce highly realistic outputs.

- **Variational Autoencoders (VAEs):** VAEs are a type of autoencoder that learns to encode input data into a latent space and then decode it back into the original format. By sampling from the latent space, VAEs can generate new data that is similar to the input data.

- **Transformers and Language Models:** Transformers, such as GPT-3 and BERT, have revolutionized natural language processing by enabling the generation of coherent and contextually relevant text. These models use attention mechanisms to understand and generate human-like language.

- **Diffusion Models:** Diffusion models are a class of generative models that learn to generate data by reversing a diffusion process. These models have shown promise in generating high-quality images and other types of data.

Applications of Generative AI

Generative AI has a wide range of applications across various industries:

- **Content Creation:** Generative AI can create written content, such as articles, stories, and poetry, as well as visual content like images and videos. This has significant implications for media, entertainment, and marketing.

- **Design and Art:** Artists and designers use generative AI to explore new creative possibilities, generate unique artworks, and design innovative products.

- **Healthcare:** In healthcare, generative AI can assist in drug discovery, medical imaging, and the creation of personalized treatment plans.

- **Gaming and Virtual Worlds:** Generative AI is used to create realistic characters, environments, and scenarios in video games and virtual reality experiences.

- **Finance:** In finance, generative AI can generate synthetic data for risk modeling, fraud detection, and algorithmic trading.

Importance of Cloud Infrastructure:

The computational demands of generative AI models are immense, requiring significant processing power, storage, and networking capabilities. Cloud infrastructure provides the necessary resources to train, deploy, and scale these models efficiently. By leveraging cloud services, organizations can access cutting-edge AI technologies without the need for extensive on-premises hardware investments.

Challenges and Future Directions
While generative AI holds great promise, it also presents several challenges:

- **Ethical Considerations:** The ability to generate realistic content raises ethical concerns, such as the potential for misuse in creating deepfakes or spreading misinformation.

- **Data Privacy:** Generative AI models often require large amounts of data, raising concerns about data privacy and security.

- **Bias and Fairness:** Ensuring that generative AI models produce fair and unbiased outputs is a significant challenge that requires ongoing research and attention.

Looking ahead, the future of generative AI is bright, with ongoing advancements in model architectures, training techniques, and applications. As we continue to explore the potential of generative AI, it is essential to address these challenges and ensure that the technology is used responsibly and ethically.

Inference

Generative AI is transforming the way we create and interact with technology, opening up new possibilities for innovation and creativity. In the following chapters, we will delve deeper into the various components of cloud infrastructure that support generative AI and learn how to harness their full potential to build the future of AI-driven applications.

Applications and Use Cases of Generative AI

Generative AI is revolutionizing various industries by enabling the creation of new content, ideas, and solutions. This chapter explores the diverse applications and use cases of generative AI, highlighting its transformative impact across different sectors.

Content Creation

Generative AI has significantly advanced the field of content creation, enabling the generation of text, images, videos, and more. Here are some key applications:

- **Text Generation:** AI models like GPT-3 can generate human-like text, making them useful for writing articles, stories, poetry, and even code. These models can assist writers by providing creative suggestions or generating entire pieces of content.

- **Image Generation:** Tools like DALL-E and GANs can create realistic images from textual descriptions. This capability is valuable for artists, designers, and marketers who need unique visuals for their projects.

- **Video Generation:** Generative AI can produce videos by synthesizing new frames from existing ones or creating entirely new sequences. This technology is used in filmmaking, advertising, and virtual reality experiences.

Design and Art

Generative AI is a powerful tool for artists and designers, offering new ways to explore creativity and innovation:

- **Art Creation:** AI-generated art has gained popularity, with artists using generative models to create unique and thought-provoking pieces. These artworks can be exhibited in galleries, sold as NFTs, or used in digital media.

- **Product Design:** Designers use generative AI to create innovative product designs, from fashion to industrial design. AI can generate multiple design variations, helping designers explore new possibilities and optimize their creations.

- **Architecture:** In architecture, generative AI can assist in designing buildings and urban landscapes. AI models can generate architectural plans, optimize layouts, and even create virtual walkthroughs of proposed structures.

Healthcare

Generative AI is making significant contributions to the healthcare industry by improving diagnostics, treatment, and research:

- **Drug Discovery:** AI models can generate potential drug candidates by analyzing vast amounts of chemical data. This accelerates the drug discovery process and helps identify new treatments for diseases.
- **Medical Imaging:** Generative AI can enhance medical images, such as MRI or CT scans, by generating high-resolution images from lower-quality inputs. This improves diagnostic accuracy and helps doctors make better-informed decisions.
- **Personalized Treatment:** AI can generate personalized treatment plans based on a patient's medical history and genetic information. This approach ensures that patients receive the most effective and tailored treatments.

Gaming and Virtual Worlds

Generative AI is transforming the gaming industry by creating more immersive and dynamic experiences:

- **Character Creation:** AI can generate realistic and diverse characters for video games, complete with unique appearances, behaviors, and backstories. This enhances the player's experience and adds depth to the game world.
- **Environment Generation:** Generative AI can create vast and detailed virtual environments, from landscapes to entire cities. This allows game developers to build expansive worlds with minimal manual effort.
- **Storytelling:** AI-driven storytelling can generate dynamic narratives that adapt to the player's choices and actions. This creates a more engaging and personalized gaming experience.

Finance

In the finance sector, generative AI is used to improve risk management, fraud detection, and investment strategies:

- **Synthetic Data Generation:** AI can generate synthetic financial data for training machine learning models. This helps improve the accuracy of predictive models without compromising sensitive information.

- **Algorithmic Trading:** Generative AI can develop and optimize trading algorithms by analyzing historical market data. This enables more effective and profitable trading strategies.

- **Fraud Detection:** AI models can generate scenarios of potential fraudulent activities, helping financial institutions identify and prevent fraud more effectively.

Marketing and Advertising

Generative AI is revolutionizing marketing and advertising by creating personalized and engaging content:

- **Ad Copy Generation:** AI can generate compelling ad copy tailored to different audiences, improving the effectiveness of marketing campaigns.

- **Visual Content Creation:** Generative AI can create eye-catching visuals for advertisements, social media posts, and marketing materials. This helps brands stand out and capture the attention of their target audience.

- **Customer Engagement:** AI-driven chatbots and virtual assistants can generate personalized responses to customer inquiries, enhancing customer engagement and satisfaction.

Inference

Generative AI is a versatile and powerful technology with applications across a wide range of industries. Its ability to create new content, optimize processes, and enhance user experiences makes it a valuable tool for innovation and growth. In the following chapters, we will delve deeper into the technical aspects of generative AI and explore how to leverage cloud infrastructure to support these applications.

Importance of Cloud Infrastructure for Generative AI

Cloud infrastructure is the backbone of modern generative AI applications, providing the necessary resources to train, deploy, and scale AI models efficiently. This chapter explores the critical role of cloud infrastructure in supporting generative AI, highlighting its benefits, key components, and best practices.

Scalability and Flexibility

One of the primary advantages of cloud infrastructure is its scalability and flexibility. Generative AI models, especially large language models (LLMs) and foundation models (FMs), require significant computational power and storage. Cloud providers offer a wide range of compute instances, including those powered by GPUs and specialized AI hardware, allowing organizations to scale their resources up or down based on demand.

- **Elastic Compute Resources:** Cloud platforms provide elastic compute resources that can be dynamically allocated and deallocated, ensuring optimal resource utilization and cost efficiency.
- **Auto-scaling:** Auto-scaling features automatically adjust the number of compute instances based on workload demands, ensuring that AI applications run smoothly without manual intervention.

Cost Efficiency

Cloud infrastructure offers cost-efficient solutions for generative AI workloads. With pay-as-you-go pricing models, organizations only pay for the resources they use, avoiding the need for significant upfront investments in hardware.

- **Cost Management Tools:** Cloud providers offer tools to monitor and manage costs, helping organizations optimize their spending and identify areas for cost savings.
- **Reserved Instances and Spot Instances:** Options like reserved instances and spot instances provide additional cost-saving opportunities by offering lower prices for long-term commitments or unused capacity.

High-Performance Computing

Generative AI models require high-performance computing (HPC) capabilities to handle complex computations and large datasets. Cloud providers offer HPC solutions that deliver the necessary processing power and speed.

- **GPU and TPU Instances:** Cloud platforms provide instances with GPUs and TPUs, which are optimized for AI and machine learning workloads, enabling faster training and inference.
- **High-Throughput Storage:** High-performance storage solutions, such as Amazon FSx for Lustre and Azure NetApp Files, ensure that data is quickly accessible for AI models.

Managed AI Services

Cloud providers offer managed AI services that simplify the deployment and management of generative AI applications. These services provide pre-built tools and frameworks, reducing the complexity of building and maintaining AI models.

- **Amazon SageMaker:** A comprehensive service for building, training, and deploying machine learning models at scale.
- **Azure Machine Learning:** A platform that provides tools for developing and deploying AI models, with support for popular frameworks like TensorFlow and PyTorch.
- **Google AI Platform:** A suite of services for building, training, and deploying AI models, with integrated support for Kubernetes and other cloud-native technologies.

Security and Compliance

Security and compliance are critical considerations for generative AI applications, especially when dealing with sensitive data. Cloud providers offer robust security features and compliance certifications to protect data and meet regulatory requirements.

- **Data Encryption:** Cloud platforms provide encryption for data at rest and in transit, ensuring that sensitive information is protected.
- **Identity and Access Management (IAM):** IAM tools help manage user access and permissions, ensuring that only authorized users can access AI resources.

- **Compliance Certifications:** Cloud providers comply with various industry standards and regulations, such as GDPR, HIPAA, and SOC 2, providing assurance that data is handled securely.

Hybrid and Multi-Cloud Strategies

Generative AI workloads often span multiple environments, including on-premises, edge, and public cloud. Hybrid and multi-cloud strategies provide flexibility and resilience, allowing organizations to leverage the best of each environment.

- **Hybrid Cloud:** Combines on-premises infrastructure with cloud resources, enabling seamless integration and data sharing.
- **Multi-Cloud:** Utilizes multiple cloud providers to avoid vendor lock-in and ensure redundancy and high availability.
- **Edge Computing:** Extends cloud capabilities to the edge, enabling low-latency processing and real-time decision-making for AI applications.

Innovation and Future Trends

Cloud infrastructure enables organizations to stay at the forefront of AI innovation by providing access to the latest technologies and tools. As generative AI continues to evolve, cloud providers are constantly updating their offerings to support new advancements.

- **AI Accelerators:** Specialized hardware, such as AWS Trainium and NVIDIA H100 GPUs, are designed to accelerate AI workloads, providing faster and more efficient processing.

- **Serverless Computing:** Serverless architecture allows organizations to run AI models without managing the underlying infrastructure, simplifying deployment and scaling.
- **AI Marketplaces:** Cloud platforms offer AI marketplaces where organizations can access pre-trained models, datasets, and AI services, accelerating development and deployment.

Inference

Cloud infrastructure is essential for the success of generative AI applications, providing the scalability, cost efficiency, high-performance computing, and security needed to support these advanced technologies. By leveraging cloud services, organizations can unlock the full potential of generative AI and drive innovation across various industries. In the following chapters, we will explore specific cloud services and best practices for building and deploying generative AI models.

CHAPTER 2
Foundations of Cloud Computing

This Chapter is an foundations of cloud computing

C loud computing is the backbone of modern technology, providing the infrastructure and services needed to support a wide range of applications, including generative AI. This chapter explores the fundamental concepts of cloud computing, its key components, and the major cloud service models.

Cloud computing has revolutionized the way we access and use technology, providing on-demand resources and services over the internet. This chapter covers the fundamental concepts of cloud computing, its key components, and the benefits it offers to individuals and organizations.

Basics of Cloud Computing

Cloud computing has revolutionized the way we access and use technology, providing on-demand resources and services over the internet. This chapter covers the fundamental concepts of cloud computing, its key components, and the benefits it offers to individuals and organizations.

What is Cloud Computing?

Cloud computing refers to the delivery of computing services, such as servers, storage, databases, networking, software, and analytics, over the internet. These services are provided by cloud service providers (CSPs) and are typically billed on a pay-as-you-go basis. Cloud computing allows users to access and use resources without the need for significant upfront investments in hardware and infrastructure.

Key Characteristics of Cloud Computing

Cloud computing is defined by several key characteristics:

On-Demand Self-Service: Users can provision and manage computing resources as needed without requiring human intervention from the service provider.

Broad Network Access: Cloud services are accessible over the internet from a wide range of devices, including laptops, smartphones, and tablets.

Resource Pooling: Cloud providers pool their resources to serve multiple customers, dynamically allocating and reallocating resources based on demand.

Rapid Elasticity: Cloud resources can be quickly scaled up or down to meet changing workload demands, providing flexibility and efficiency.

Measured Service: Cloud usage is monitored, controlled, and reported, allowing users to pay only for the resources they consume.

Cloud Service Models

Cloud service models in cloud computing refer to the standardized framework functioning for delivering computing resources and services on the internet. It defines the structure and component framework defining the way services are offered, managed, and delivered.

Cloud service models provide businesses and individuals with different levels of control, responsibility, and management over IT resources. This allows them to choose the most suitable approach based on their own needs and capabilities.

Cloud computing services are typically categorized into three main models:

Infrastructure as a Service (IaaS): IaaS provides virtualized computing resources over the internet. Users can rent virtual machines, storage, and networking components, allowing them to build and manage their own IT infrastructure. Examples of IaaS providers include Amazon Web Services (AWS), Microsoft Azure, and Google Cloud Platform (GCP).

Platform as a Service (PaaS): PaaS offers a platform that allows developers to build, deploy, and manage applications without worrying about the underlying infrastructure. PaaS provides tools and frameworks for application development, as well as managed services for databases, storage, and networking. Examples of PaaS providers include AWS Elastic Beanstalk, Azure App Service, and Google App Engine.

Software as a Service (SaaS): SaaS delivers software applications over the internet on a subscription basis. Users can access and use the software through a web browser, without needing to install or maintain it on their local devices. Examples of SaaS applications include Microsoft Office 365, Google Workspace, and Salesforce.

Key Components of Cloud Computing

Cloud computing consists of several key components that work together to deliver services:

Compute: The processing power needed to run applications and perform computations. This includes virtual machines, containers, and serverless computing.

Storage: The capacity to store data, including databases, object storage, and file storage. Cloud storage solutions provide scalable and durable storage options.

Networking: The infrastructure that connects cloud resources and enables data transfer. This includes virtual networks, load balancers, and content delivery networks (CDNs).

Security: Measures to protect data and applications in the cloud, including encryption, identity and access management (IAM), and compliance with industry standards and regulations.

Benefits of Cloud Computing

Cloud computing offers numerous benefits for individuals and organizations: Cost Savings: Cloud computing eliminates the need for significant upfront investments in hardware and infrastructure, allowing users to pay only for the resources they use.

Scalability: Cloud services can be easily scaled up or down to meet changing demands, providing flexibility and efficiency.

Accessibility: Cloud services are accessible from anywhere with an internet connection, enabling remote work and collaboration.

Reliability: Cloud providers offer high levels of reliability and availability, with built-in redundancy and disaster recovery capabilities.

Innovation: Cloud platforms provide access to the latest technologies and tools, enabling organizations to innovate and stay competitive.

Challenges and Considerations

While cloud computing offers many advantages, it also presents several challenges and considerations:

Security: Ensuring the security of data and applications in the cloud is a critical concern. Organizations must implement robust security measures and comply with industry standards and regulations.

Data Privacy: Protecting sensitive data and maintaining privacy is essential, especially when dealing with personal or confidential information.

Vendor Lock-In: Relying on a single cloud provider can lead to vendor lock-in, making it difficult to switch providers or adopt a multi-cloud strategy.

Cost Management: Managing cloud costs can be challenging, especially with the complexity of pricing models and the potential for unexpected expenses.

Inference

Understanding the basics of cloud computing is essential for leveraging its full potential in generative AI and other applications. By exploring the key characteristics, service models, components, benefits, and challenges of cloud computing, individuals and organizations can make informed decisions and build robust, scalable, and cost-effective cloud solutions. In the following chapters, we will delve deeper into specific cloud services and best practices for building and deploying generative AI models.

Key Cloud Service Models

Cloud computing offers a variety of service models that cater to different needs and use cases. Understanding these models is essential for leveraging the full potential of cloud infrastructure. This chapter explores the three primary cloud service models: Infrastructure as a Service (IaaS), Platform as a Service (PaaS), Software as a Service (SaaS).

Let's take a look at the following diagram which visualizes the different models, and their differing levels of responsibility then examine each of the options in further detail below.

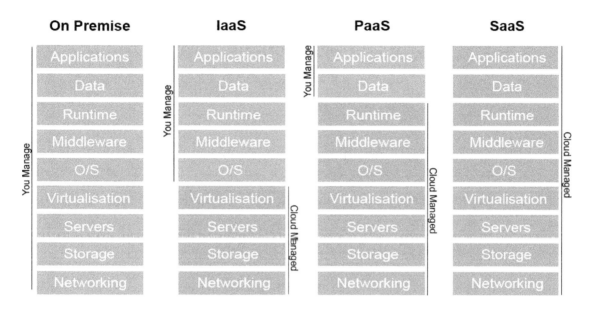

Infrastructure as a Service (IaaS):

Provides virtualized computing resources over the internet. It offers fundamental building blocks for IT infrastructure, allowing users to rent virtual machines, storage, and networking components. IaaS is ideal for organizations that want to maintain control over their infrastructure while avoiding the costs and complexities of managing physical hardware.

Characteristics

- IAAS provides virtualized computing resources such as virtual machines, storage, and networking components.
- Scale resources up or down based on demand, avoiding over-provisioning and minimizing costs.
- Users can manage and configure resources independently through a web interface or API.

- **Key Features of IaaS:**
    - **Virtual Machines (VMs):** Users can create and manage VMs with customizable configurations, including PU, memory, and storage.

    - **Storage:** Scalable storage solutions, such as block storage, object storage, and file storage, are available to meet various data needs.

    - **Networking:** Virtual networks, load balancers, and VPNs enable secure and efficient data transfer.

    - **Scalability:** IaaS allows users to scale resources up or down based on demand, ensuring optimal performance and cost efficiency.

    - **Pay-as-You-Go Pricing:** Users pay only for the resources they consume, making IaaS a cost-effective solution.

- **Examples of IaaS Providers:**
    - **Amazon Web Services (AWS):** Offers a wide range of IaaS services, including EC2 (Elastic Compute Cloud), EBS (Elastic Block Store), and VPC (Virtual Private Cloud).

- o **Microsoft Azure:** Provides IaaS services such as Azure Virtual Machines, Azure Blob Storage, and Azure Virtual Network.

- o **Google Cloud Platform (GCP):** Offers IaaS services like Compute Engine, Cloud Storage, and Virtual Private Cloud (VPC).

Benefits

- Eliminate the need for upfront hardware investment and reduce operational costs.
- Customize virtual environments to match specific requirements, enhancing performance and resource utilization.
- Instantly deploy and configure virtual instances, accelerating application development and testing.

Platform as a Service (PaaS)

provides a platform that allows developers to build, deploy, and manage applications without worrying about the underlying infrastructure. PaaS offers tools and frameworks for application development, as well as managed services for databases, storage, and networking. This model is ideal for developers who want to focus on coding and innovation rather than infrastructure management.

Characteristics

- PAAS provides a platform with tools, libraries, and frameworks for cloud application development.

- Management of underlying infrastructure, including hardware and operating systems, is abstracted.
- Developers can collaborate on projects within the platform, promoting teamwork and efficient development.

- **Key Features of PaaS:**

  - **Development Tools:** Integrated development environments (IDEs), version control systems, and collaboration tools streamline the development process.

  - **Application Hosting:** PaaS platforms provide hosting environments for web and mobile applications, ensuring high availability and scalability.

  - **Database Management:** Managed database services, such as SQL and NoSQL databases, simplify data storage and retrieval.

  - **Middleware:** PaaS includes middleware services, such as messaging and integration, to support application functionality.

  - **Security and Compliance:** Built-in security features and compliance certifications help protect applications and data.

- **Examples of PaaS Providers:**

  - **AWS Elastic Beanstalk**: A PaaS service that simplifies the deployment and management of applications using popular programming languages and frameworks.

  - **Azure App Service:** A PaaS offering that enables developers to build and host web apps, mobile apps, and APIs in the cloud.

  - **Google App Engine:** A fully managed PaaS that allows developers to build and deploy applications using various programming languages and frameworks.

Benefits
- Focus on code and application logic without worrying about infrastructure management.
- Rapidly deploy applications with built-in development, testing, and deployment tools.
- Easily scale applications based on traffic and demand, enhancing user experience.

Software as a Service (SaaS)

Software as a Service (SaaS) delivers software applications over the internet on a subscription basis. Users can access and use the software through a web browser, without needing to install or maintain it on their local devices. SaaS is ideal for organizations and individuals who want to use software without the hassle of managing infrastructure or updates.

Characteristics

- SAAS offers ready-to-use applications hosted on the cloud and accessible via the Internet.
- Subscription based application on cloud environment, eliminating the need for upfront licensing fees.
- Service providers handle maintenance, updates, and security patches.

- **Key Features of SaaS:**
  - **Accessibility:** SaaS applications are accessible from any device with an internet connection, enabling remote work and collaboration.
  - **Automatic Updates:** SaaS providers handle software updates and maintenance, ensuring that users always have access to the latest features and security patches.

  - **Scalability:** SaaS applications can scale to accommodate a growing number of users and increased workload demands.

- o **Subscription-Based Pricing:** Users pay a subscription fee, typically on a monthly or annual basis, making SaaS a cost-effective solution.

- o **Integration:** SaaS applications often integrate with other software and services, providing a seamless user experience.

- **Examples of SaaS Providers:**
  - o **Microsoft Office 365:** A suite of productivity applications, including Word, Excel, and PowerPoint, accessible through the cloud.

  - o **Google Workspace:** A collection of cloud-based productivity and collaboration tools, such as Gmail, Google Drive, and Google Docs.

  - o **Salesforce:** A cloud-based customer relationship management (CRM) platform that helps businesses manage sales, marketing, and customer service.

Benefits

- Access applications from anywhere with an internet connection, promoting remote work and collaboration.
- Predictable subscription costs make budgeting and financial planning easier.

- Quickly deploy and use software without lengthy installation processes.

Comparing IaaS, PaaS, and SaaS

Feature	IaaS	PaaS	SaaS
Control	High (infrastructure management)	Medium (application development)	Low (software usage)
Flexibility	High (customizable resources)	Medium(pre-configured platform)	Low (pre-built software)
Maintenance	User-managed	Shared (user and provider)	Provider-managed
Use Case	Custom IT infrastructure	Application development and deployment	Software access and usage
Examples	AWS EC2, Azure VMs, Google Compute Engine	AWS Elastic Beanstalk, Azure App Service	Microsoft Office 365, Google Workspace

Inference

Understanding the key cloud service models—Infrastructure as a Service (IaaS), Platform as a Service (PaaS), and Software as a Service (SaaS)—is essential for leveraging the full potential of cloud computing. Each model offers unique benefits and use cases, allowing organizations to choose the best solution for their needs. In the following chapters, we will explore specific cloud services and best practices for building and deploying generative AI models.

Major Cloud Providers (AWS, Azure, Google Cloud)

The cloud computing landscape is dominated by three major providers: Amazon Web Services (AWS), Microsoft Azure, and Google Cloud Platform (GCP). Each of these providers offers a comprehensive suite of services and solutions to meet the diverse needs of businesses and developers. This chapter explores the key features, services, and strengths of these leading cloud providers.

Amazon Web Services (AWS):

AWS is the largest and most comprehensive cloud provider, offering a vast array of services across computing, storage, databases, machine learning, and more. AWS is known for its scalability, reliability, and global reach.

Key Features and Services:

- **Compute:** AWS offers a wide range of compute services, including EC2 (Elastic Compute Cloud) for virtual servers, Lambda for serverless computing, and ECS/EKS for container orchestration.

- **Storage:** AWS provides scalable storage solutions such as S3 (Simple Storage Service) for object storage, EBS (Elastic Block Store) for block storage, and Glacier for archival storage.

- **Databases**: AWS offers managed database services, including RDS (Relational Database Service) for SQL databases, DynamoDB for NoSQL databases, and Redshift for data warehousing.

- **Machine Learning:** AWS provides a suite of AI and machine learning services, including SageMaker for building and deploying machine learning models, Rekognition for image and video analysis, and

Comprehend for natural language processing, Amazon Bedrock A fully managed service that makes foundational models (FMs) from Amazon and leading AI startups available through an AP

- **Networking:** AWS offers networking services such as VPC (Virtual Private Cloud) for isolated network environments, CloudFront for content delivery, and Route 53 for DNS management.
- **Security:** AWS provides robust security features, including IAM (Identity and Access Management), KMS (Key Management Service) for encryption, and GuardDuty for threat detection.

Strengths:

- **Global Infrastructure:** AWS has a vast global infrastructure with data centers in multiple regions, ensuring low latency and high availability.
- **Ecosystem:** AWS has a rich ecosystem of services and third-party integrations, making it a versatile platform for various use cases.
- **Innovation:** AWS continuously innovates and introduces new services and features, staying at the forefront of cloud technology.

Microsoft Azure:

Azure is a leading cloud platform that provides a wide range of services for computing, storage, databases, AI, and IoT. Azure is known for its strong integration with Microsoft products and services, as well as its hybrid cloud capabilities.

Key Features and Services:

- **Compute:** Azure offers virtual machines, Azure Functions for serverless computing, and Azure Kubernetes Service (AKS) for container orchestration.
- **Storage:** Azure provides storage solutions such as Blob Storage for object storage, Azure Files for file storage, and Azure Disk Storage for block storage.
- **Databases:** Azure offers managed database services, including Azure SQL Database, Cosmos DB for NoSQL databases, and Azure Synapse Analytics for data warehousing.
- **AI and Machine Learning:** Azure provides AI and machine learning services, including Azure Machine Learning for building and deploying models, Cognitive Services for pre-built AI capabilities, and Bot Service for building conversational agents.
- **Networking:** Azure offers networking services such as Virtual Network, Azure CDN for content delivery, and Azure DNS for domain management.
- **Security:** Azure provides comprehensive security features, including Azure Active Directory for identity management, Azure Security Center for threat protection, and Azure Key Vault for encryption.

Strengths:

- **Integration with Microsoft Products:** Azure seamlessly integrates with Microsoft products such as Windows Server, SQL Server, and Office 365, making it an attractive choice for organizations already using Microsoft technologies.

- **Hybrid Cloud:** Azure's hybrid cloud capabilities, including Azure Arc and Azure Stack, enable organizations to manage and deploy resources across on-premises, edge, and cloud environments.
- **Enterprise Focus:** Azure offers enterprise-grade solutions and support, making it a preferred choice for large organizations and enterprises.

Google Cloud Platform (GCP)

GCP offers a suite of cloud services, including computing, storage, databases, machine learning, and data analytics. GCP is known for its advanced data and AI capabilities, as well as its focus on open-source technologies.

Key Features and Services:

Compute: GCP offers Compute Engine for virtual machines, Cloud Functions for serverless computing, and Google Kubernetes Engine (GKE) for container orchestration.

Storage: GCP provides storage solutions such as Cloud Storage for object storage, Persistent Disks for block storage, and Filestore for file storage.

Databases: GCP offers managed database services, including Cloud SQL for relational databases, Firestore for NoSQL databases, and BigQuery for data warehousing and analytics.

AI and Machine Learning: GCP provides AI and machine learning services, including AI Platform for building and deploying models, Vision AI for image analysis, and Natural Language AI for text analysis.

Networking: GCP offers networking services such as Virtual Private Cloud (VPC), Cloud CDN for content delivery, and Cloud DNS for domain management.

Security: GCP provides robust security features, including Identity and Access Management (IAM), Cloud Key Management for encryption, and Security Command Center for threat detection.

Strengths:

Data and AI Capabilities: GCP excels in data analytics and AI, offering powerful tools and services for data processing, machine learning, and artificial intelligence.

Open-Source Commitment: GCP has a strong commitment to open-source technologies, supporting projects such as Kubernetes, TensorFlow, and Apache Beam.

Innovation: GCP continuously innovates and introduces new services and features, particularly in the areas of data analytics and AI.

Comparing AWS, Azure, and GCP

Feature	AWS	Azure	GCP
Compute	EC2, Lambda, ECS/EKS	Virtual Machines, Azure Functions, AKS	Compute Engine, Cloud Functions, GKE
Storage	S3, EBS, Glacier	Blob Storage, Azure Files, Disk Storage	Cloud Storage, Persistent Disks, Filestore
Databases	RDS, DynamoDB, Redshift	Azure SQL Database, Cosmos DB, Synapse	Cloud SQL, Firestore, BigQuery

AI and Machine Learning	SageMaker, Rekognition, Comprehend	Azure Machine Learning, Cognitive Services	AI Platform, Vision AI, Natural Language AI
Networking	VPC, CloudFront, Route 53	Virtual Network, Azure CDN, Azure DNS	VPC, Cloud CDN, Cloud DNS
Security	IAM, KMS, GuardDuty	Azure Active Directory, Security Center	IAM, Cloud Key Management, Security Command Center
Strengths	Global reach, rich ecosystem, innovation	Integration with Microsoft products, hybrid cloud, enterprise focus	Data and AI capabilities, open-source commitment, innovation

Inference

AWS, Azure, and GCP are the leading cloud providers, each offering a comprehensive suite of services and solutions to meet the diverse needs of businesses and developers. By understanding the key features, services, and strengths of these providers, organizations can make informed decisions and choose the best cloud platform for their specific requirements. In the following chapters, we will explore specific cloud services and best practices for building and deploying generative AI models.

CHAPTER 3
Compute Resources for Generative AI

This Chapter all about Understanding of Compute Resources for Generative AI

G enerative AI models, such as Generative Adversarial Networks (GANs), Variational Autoencoders (VAEs), and large language models like GPT, are computationally intensive. The success of these models depends heavily on the availability of robust and scalable compute resources. This chapter discusses the various compute options available, their benefits, and best practices for leveraging them effectively

The Role of Compute Power in AI Development

Compute power allows AI systems to perform a series of intensive operations necessary for tasks like training deep learning models. These models are built by processing enormous datasets, often requiring multiple iterations to improve accuracy. The more computational resources available, the faster these models can be trained. Without sufficient processing capability, AI development slows considerably, making it difficult to deploy models on time or at the required performance levels.

For example, the development of autonomous vehicles depends on AI models trained on millions of images and hours of video footage. Processing this data efficiently requires high-performance GPUs (Graphics Processing Units) to run multiple operations in parallel. Similarly, AI-powered chatbots that provide real-time customer service use compute resources to analyze incoming messages and generate relevant responses instantaneously.

Computational limitations can also restrict the capabilities of AI models. Smaller models that use limited compute power may struggle to deliver the same accuracy as larger ones. This makes high-performance computing essential not only for developing more advanced systems but also for ensuring reliability in real-world applications.

Types of Compute Resources

Cloud infrastructure provides a variety of compute resources tailored for different workloads and performance requirements. These include:

- Virtual Machines (VMs)
- Containers
- Serverless Computing
- Dedicated Hardware (e.g., GPUs, TPUs)

1. Virtual Machines (VMs):

Virtual Machines are virtualized instances of physical hardware. They provide a flexible and scalable environment for running AI workloads.

Advantages:

- **Scalability:** Easily scale up or down based on workload demands.
- **Customization:** Full control over the operating system, software stack, and configurations.
- **Isolation:** Each VM operates in isolation, providing security and reliability.

Use Cases:

- Suitable for training medium-sized models and running inferencing tasks.

- Ideal for environments that require specific configurations and custom libraries.

2. Containers

Containers are lightweight, portable, and consistent environments for running applications. They package the application code, dependencies, and configurations into a single unit.

Advantages:

- **Portability:** Run consistently across different environments.
- **Efficiency:** Consume fewer resources compared to VMs.
- **Scalability:** Easily scale out by deploying multiple containers.

Use Cases:

- Ideal for deploying and scaling AI inference services.
- Suitable for microservices architectures and DevOps practices.

3. Serverless Computing

Serverless computing abstracts the underlying infrastructure, allowing developers to focus solely on the application code. AWS Lambda is a popular serverless compute service.

Advantages:

- **No Infrastructure Management:** Automatic scaling and management of resources.
- **Cost Efficiency:** Pay only for the actual compute time consumed.
- **Quick Deployment:** Simplifies deployment and reduces time to market.

Use Cases:

- Suitable for event-driven workloads and real-time inferencing.
- Ideal for applications with unpredictable or sporadic usage patterns.

4. Dedicated Hardware GPUs/TPUs

Generative AI models require significant computational power, especially for training. Graphics Processing Units (GPUs) and Tensor Processing Units (TPUs) are specialized hardware designed to accelerate AI workloads.

Advantages:

- **High Performance:** Accelerate training and inference with parallel processing capabilities.
- **Efficiency:** Handle large volumes of data and complex computations efficiently.
- **Optimized for AI:** Specifically designed to meet the demands of AI and deep learning models.

Use Cases:

- Essential for training large-scale generative models like GANs and VAEs.
- Ideal for deploying high-throughput, low-latency inference services.

Types of Compute Infrastructure Supporting AI

AI models rely on several types of infrastructure, each suited for specific use cases. Below are the most common types of infrastructure and their roles in AI development:

- ## High-Performance Computing (HPC)

  HPC systems combine multiple processors to tackle intensive tasks, such as training large machine learning models. Research institutions and enterprises often use HPC clusters to process vast datasets efficiently. For example, pharmaceutical companies use HPC to model drug interactions, while financial institutions rely on it for fraud detection algorithms.

- ## GPUs/TPUs/ FPGAs

  Three types of processors or different types of compute resources are essential in AI development, with GPUs offering flexibility and TPUs providing faster performance for targeted applications.

  - **GPUs:** Graphics Processing Units excel at handling the parallel computations required for deep learning. These processors are widely used in fields such as computer vision and natural language processing.

- o **Advantages:**
  - **High Performance:** Significantly faster than CPUs for training and inference of deep learning models.
  - **Parallel Processing:** Capable of performing thousands of parallel operations, making them ideal for the matrix and vector operations common in AI.

- o **Use Cases:**
  - **Training Deep Learning Models:** Essential for training large and complex models such as GANs, VAEs, and transformers.
  - **High-Throughput Inference:** Ideal for applications requiring real-time inference, such as video analysis and autonomous driving.

- o **Examples:**
  - **NVIDIA Tesla V100:** A powerful GPU designed specifically for AI and deep learning workloads.
  - **NVIDIA A100:** Built for AI acceleration, offering exceptional performance for both training and inference

- **TPUs:** Tensor Processing Units, developed by Google, are optimized specifically for machine learning workloads. They offer higher efficiency for specific AI tasks, such as training large neural networks.
    - Advantages:
        - **Optimized for AI:** Designed from the ground up to handle the specific requirements of machine learning model
        - **Energy Efficient:** Consume less power compared to GPUs while delivering comparable performance.
    - Use Cases:
        - **Training Large-Scale Models:** Suitable for training state-of-the-art models in a fraction of the time it would take on CPUs or GPUs.
        - **High-Efficiency Inference:** Ideal for serving models in production environments where efficiency is crucial.
    - Examples:
        - **Google TPU v3:** Offers significant computational power for large-scale model training.
        - **Google TPU v4:** The latest generation of TPUs, providing even higher performance for advanced AI workloads.
- **FPGAs**

    FPGAs are integrated circuits that can be configured by the user after manufacturing. They offer a unique balance between performance and flexibility, allowing for custom hardware configurations.

- o **Advantages:**
  - **Customizability:** Can be tailored to specific workloads and algorithms, providing optimized performance for unique applications.

  - **Low Latency:** Provides real-time processing capabilities, making them suitable for applications requiring immediate responses.

  - **Energy Efficiency:** Offers high performance per watt, making them suitable for energy-sensitive applications.

- o **Use Cases**
  - **Edge Computing:** Ideal for deploying AI models at the edge, where low latency and high efficiency are crucial.
  - **Custom AI Accelerators:** Used in specialized AI applications that require custom hardware configurations for optimal performance.

- o **Example**

- **Xilinx Alveo U250:** A high-performance FPGA designed for data center and AI applications, providing the flexibility to accelerate a wide range of workloads.

Comparative Analysis
- **Performance**
  - **GPUs:** Provide high performance for training and inference, ideal for parallel processing.
  - **TPUs:** Optimized for AI, offering high performance and efficiency for large-scale models.
  - **FPGAs:** Offer customizable performance, suitable for specialized and low-latency applications.

- **Cost Efficiency**
  - **GPUs**: Higher cost but justified by their performance for complex AI workloads.
  - **TPUs:** Cost-efficient for large-scale training, offering a balance between cost and performance.
  - **FPGAs:** Cost can vary based on customization but offers efficiency for specific use cases.

- **Scalability**
  - **GPUs:** Scales well for parallel processing tasks.
  - **TPUs:** Designed for large-scale deployment, easily scalable across multiple units.

- **FPGAs:** Scalability depends on the specific application and customization requirements.

• Cloud Computing

Cloud platforms like AWS, Google Cloud, and Microsoft Azure allow organizations to rent compute power as needed. This flexibility makes it easier for companies to scale AI projects without investing in expensive on-premise infrastructure. Cloud services are particularly useful for startups and smaller teams that require access to powerful tools without high upfront costs.

- **Amazon Web Services (AWS)**
  AWS offers a wide range of services tailored for AI workloads, providing flexibility and scalability for various use cases.
  - **Amazon EC2:** Provides scalable virtual machines with GPU and FPGA options. Instances like p3 (NVIDIA V100 GPUs) and p4 (NVIDIA A100 GPUs) are designed for deep learning workloads.

  - **Amazon SageMaker:** A fully managed service that covers the entire machine learning lifecycle, from data preparation to model deployment.

  - **AWS Lambda:** Serverless computing for running code in response to events, suitable for event-driven AI applications.

- **Microsoft Azure**

  Azure provides a comprehensive suite of AI and compute services, enabling the development and deployment of sophisticated AI models.

  - **Azure Virtual Machines:** Scalable VMs with GPU support for high-performance computing tasks.

  - **Azure Machine Learning:** A platform for building, training, and deploying machine learning models, with integrated tools for collaboration and monitoring.

  - **Azure Functions:** Serverless computing for executing code in response to events, ideal for real-time AI processing.

- **Google Cloud Platform (GCP)**

  GCP offers robust AI and compute services, designed to meet the needs of both researchers and enterprises.

  - **Google Compute Engine:** Customizable VMs with GPU and TPU options, supporting a range of AI workloads**.**

  - **Google AI Platform**: A suite of tools for developing, training, and deploying machine learning models, with support for advanced features like hyperparameter tuning and automated model deployment.

- ○ **Cloud Functions:** Serverless execution for event-driven code, enabling real-time AI applications.

- # Edge Computing

Edge computing involves processing data locally, closer to where it is generated, rather than relying on centralized servers. This method reduces latency, which is critical for real-time applications like self-driving cars or IoT devices.

Choosing the Right Compute Resources

Selecting the appropriate compute resources depends on several factors:

- **Model Complexity:** Larger and more complex models benefit from GPUs and TPUs.
- **Workload Type:** Training requires high-performance compute resources, while inference can be served with VMs or containers.
- **Scalability Needs:** Consider serverless for sporadic or unpredictable workloads, and containers for scalable and portable deployments.
- **Cost Constraints:** Balance performance requirements with budget considerations. Utilize cost-optimization strategies, such as using spot instances for non-critical workloads and reserved instances for long-term, stable workloads.

Best Practices for Using Compute Resources

To maximize the efficiency and effectiveness of compute resources, consider the following best practices:

- **Monitor and Optimize:** Continuously monitor resource usage with tools like AWS CloudWatch, Azure Monitor, and GCP Stackdriver. Optimize configurations based on performance metrics.

- **Leverage Spot Instances:** Use spot instances for cost savings on non-critical workloads. Spot instances offer spare cloud capacity at a lower price.

- **Leverage Managed Services**: Utilize cloud provider services like AWS SageMaker, Google AI Platform, and Azure Machine Learning for simplified management.

- **Hybrid Approach:** Combine different compute resources, such as using CPUs for preprocessing and GPUs/TPUs for training, to meet diverse workload requirements. Use the right mix of GPUs, TPUs, and FPGAs to optimize performance and cost.

- **Automate Scaling:** Implement auto-scaling mechanisms to handle dynamic workload demands. Services like AWS Auto Scaling, Azure Scale Sets, and GCP Autoscaler can help manage resource scaling automatically.

Advanced Considerations

Distributed Training

For very large models and datasets, distributed training across multiple machines can significantly reduce training time. Frameworks like Horovod and TensorFlow's tf.distribute.Strategy facilitate distributed training.

Model Parallelism vs. Data Parallelism

- **Model Parallelism:** Splits the model itself across multiple devices, useful for very large models that can't fit into the memory of a single device.

- **Data Parallelism:** Splits the data across multiple devices, each device training a copy of the model. This is the most common approach for distributed training.

Inference

Understanding the various compute resources available for generative AI is crucial for building, training, and deploying effective AI models. By selecting the right resources and following best practices, organizations can harness the full potential of generative AI while optimizing performance and cost.

Specialized AI Hardware

Generative AI models demand immense computational power, often exceeding the capabilities of traditional hardware. Specialized AI hardware, such as AWS Trainium and NVIDIA H100, provides the performance and efficiency required to train and deploy these sophisticated models. This chapter explores the key features, benefits, and applications of AWS Trainium and NVIDIA H100.

AWS Trainium:

AWS Trainium is a custom machine learning chip designed by AWS to deliver high performance and cost-efficiency for training deep learning models. It is integrated into Amazon EC2 Trn1 instances, making it accessible for a wide range of AI workloads.

Key Features

- **High Performance:** AWS Trainium offers up to 50% lower cost-to-train compared to other comparable Amazon EC2 instances, making it highly cost-effective for large-scale training.

- **Scalability:** Each Trn1 instance supports up to 16 Trainium chips, enabling parallel processing and significant scalability.

- **Optimized for Machine Learning:** Trainium is designed specifically for machine learning workloads, offering optimized performance for both training and inference.

Use Cases

- **Natural Language Processing (NLP):** Ideal for training large language models, such as GPT and BERT, which require significant computational resources.

- **Computer Vision:** Suitable for training deep learning models for image recognition, object detection, and other computer vision tasks.

- **Recommender Systems:** Effective for training models that power personalized recommendations, such as those used in e-commerce and content platforms.

Example

Amazon EC2 Trn1 Instances: Trn1 instances, powered by AWS Trainium, are designed to deliver high performance and cost savings for training deep learning models. These instances are available in various sizes to meet different workload requirements.

NVIDIA H100:

NVIDIA H100 is part of NVIDIA's Hopper architecture and represents the latest generation of GPUs designed for AI and high-performance computing (HPC). The H100 is engineered to deliver exceptional performance for both training and inference of AI models.

Key Features

- **Unmatched Performance:** The H100 provides significant performance improvements over its predecessors, making it ideal for the most demanding AI workloads.

- **Energy Efficiency:** Designed with energy efficiency in mind, the H100 offers high performance per watt, reducing operational costs.

- **Scalability:** Supports large-scale deployments in data centers and can be integrated into high-performance computing clusters.

Use Cases

- **Training Large-Scale Models:** Suitable for training the most complex models, including large language models and deep learning networks.

- **High-Throughput Inference:** Ideal for applications requiring real-time inference, such as autonomous vehicles, robotics, and edge AI.

- **Scientific Computing:** Effective for high-performance computing tasks in scientific research, including simulations and data analysis.

Example

NVIDIA DGX H100 Systems: The DGX H100 systems integrate multiple H100 GPUs, providing a turnkey solution for AI research and development. These systems are designed to deliver optimal performance and scalability for AI and HPC workloads.

Comparative Analysis

Performance:

- **AWS Trainium:** Optimized for cost-effective training of deep learning models, offering high performance and scalability.

- **NVIDIA H100:** Delivers unmatched performance for both training and inference, suitable for the most demanding AI and HPC workloads.

Cost Efficiency

- **AWS Trainium:** Provides significant cost savings for training, with up to 50% lower cost-to-train compared to other EC2 instances.

- **NVIDIA H100:** While highly performant, the H100's cost can be higher due to its advanced capabilities and energy efficiency.

Scalability

- **AWS Trainium:** Scales effectively with up to 16 Trainium chips per Trn1 instance, suitable for large-scale training tasks.

- **NVIDIA H100:** Scales across multiple GPUs and can be integrated into high-performance computing clusters for large-scale deployments.

Best Practices for Leveraging Specialized AI Hardware

To maximize the benefits of specialized AI hardware, consider the following best practices:

- **Profile Workloads:** Analyze your AI workloads to determine which hardware best meets your performance and cost requirements.

- **Optimize Data Pipelines:** Ensure efficient data transfer and storage to keep the hardware fully utilized.

- **Leverage Managed Services:** Utilize managed services like AWS SageMaker and NVIDIA GPU Cloud for easier setup and management of AI workloads.

- **Monitor and Adjust:** Continuously monitor performance metrics and adjust configurations to optimize resource usage and cost.

Inference

Specialized AI hardware, such as AWS Trainium and NVIDIA H100, provides the performance and efficiency required for training and deploying advanced generative AI models. By understanding their features, benefits, and use cases, organizations can select the right hardware to meet their AI goals and drive innovation.

Scaling Compute Resources

Scaling compute resources is essential for managing the increasing demands of generative AI workloads. Whether training large models or deploying real-time inference services, effective scaling ensures that you can meet performance requirements while optimizing costs. This chapter explores the various strategies and best practices for scaling compute resources in cloud environments.

Understanding Scalability

Scalability refers to the ability of a system to handle growing workloads by increasing its capacity. In the context of compute resources, it involves adding more computational power or optimizing existing resources to meet the demands of AI workloads.

- **Vertical Scaling**

  Vertical scaling, also known as scaling up, involves adding more power to an existing machine, such as increasing CPU, memory, or adding more powerful GPUs.

  - **Advantages:**
    - **Simplicity:** Easier to implement as it involves upgrading a single machine.
    - **Consistency:** Maintains a single environment, reducing complexity.
  - **Disadvantages:**

- **Limits:** There is a physical limit to how much a single machine can be upgraded.
- **Cost:** Upgrading to high-end hardware can be expensive.

- **Horizontal Scaling**

  Horizontal scaling, also known as scaling out, involves adding more machines to handle increased load. This approach distributes the workload across multiple instances.

  - **Advantages:**
    - **Flexibility**: Easily add or remove instances based on demand.
    - **Fault Tolerance**: Distributed architecture can improve reliability and fault tolerance.
  - **Disadvantages:**
    - **Complexity:** Requires managing a distributed system, which can be more complex.
    - **Network Latency:** Increased communication overhead between instances.

- **Auto Scaling**

  Auto scaling automates the process of adding or removing compute resources based on real-time workload demands. Most cloud providers offer auto scaling services that help optimize resource utilization and cost.

  Amazon Web Services (AWS) Auto Scaling

AWS Auto Scaling monitors your applications and automatically adjusts capacity to maintain steady, predictable performance. It works with Amazon EC2 instances, ECS clusters, and more.

- Features:
  - **Dynamic Scaling:** Adjusts based on real-time metrics.
  - **Predictive Scaling:** Uses machine learning to anticipate traffic and scale in advance.

Microsoft Azure Scale Sets

Azure Virtual Machine Scale Sets allow you to create and manage a group of load-balanced VMs. They support auto-scaling based on metrics such as CPU, memory usage, and custom metrics.

- Features:
  - **Integration with Azure Monitor**: Automatically scale based on insights and metrics.
  - **Custom Scaling Policies**: Define custom rules for scaling based on specific needs.

Google Cloud Platform (GCP) Autoscaler

GCP Autoscaler automatically increases or decreases the number of VM instances in response to your application's demands. It integrates seamlessly with Google Kubernetes Engine (GKE) and Compute Engine.

- Features:
  - **Target Utilization Levels:** Scale based on maintaining target CPU utilization or other metrics.
  - **Integration with GKE:** Automatically scale Kubernetes clusters.

Distributed Training

For very large models and datasets, distributed training across multiple machines can significantly reduce training time. There are two main types of parallelism used in distributed training:

- **Data Parallelism**

  In data parallelism, the dataset is divided into smaller batches, and each batch is processed by a different machine running a copy of the model. The results are then aggregated.

  - **Advantages:**
    - **Scalability**: Easily scales by adding more machines.
    - **Efficiency**: Utilizes multiple machines to process data in parallel.
  - **Disadvantages:**
    - **Synchronization Overhead**: Requires synchronization of model updates, which can introduce communication overhead.

- **Model Parallelism**

  In model parallelism, the model itself is divided across multiple machines. Each machine processes a portion of the model.

  - **Advantages:**
    - **Memory Efficiency**: Allows training of very large models that don't fit into the memory of a single machine.
    - **Performance**: Can lead to performance gains for large models.

- Disadvantages:
    - **Complexity**: More complex to implement and manage compared to data parallelism.
    - **Communication Overhead**: Increased communication between machines.

Best Practices for Scaling Compute Resources

To ensure efficient scaling of compute resources, follow these best practices:

- **Monitor Performance**: Continuously monitor resource utilization using tools like AWS CloudWatch, Azure Monitor, and Google Stackdriver.
- **Optimize Resource Allocation**: Use right-sizing tools to optimize resource allocation and avoid over-provisioning.
- **Implement Auto Scaling**: Leverage auto scaling features provided by cloud providers to dynamically adjust resources based on demand.
- **Utilize Spot Instances**: For non-critical workloads, use spot instances to reduce costs.
- **Load Balancing**: Distribute incoming traffic across multiple instances to ensure even resource utilization and high availability.

Inference

Effective scaling of compute resources is crucial for managing the demands of generative AI workloads. By leveraging vertical and horizontal scaling, auto scaling features, and distributed training techniques, organizations can ensure optimal performance and cost-efficiency. Following best practices for scaling compute resources will help you meet the growing demands of AI applications while maintaining reliability and scalability.

CHAPTER 4
Storage and network Solutions for AI Workloads

A I workloads, especially those involving generative models, require efficient and scalable storage and network solutions to handle vast amounts of data and ensure high-performance computing. This chapter explores the different types of storage and network solutions in cloud environments, their benefits, use cases, and best practices for optimizing these resources.

Types of Storage Solutions

Object Storage

Object storage is designed to handle large amounts of unstructured data. It stores data as objects, each with its own metadata and unique identifier.

Cloud object storage examples

- Amazon S3 (Simple Storage Service)
- Google Cloud Storage
- Azure Blob Storage

Advantages of Object storage:

- **Scalability:** Easily scales to store vast amounts of data.
- **Durability:** Provides high durability through data replication across multiple locations.
- **Cost-Effective**: Generally more cost-effective for storing large datasets.

Use Cases:

- **Raw Data Storage:** Ideal for storing raw data such as images, videos, and large datasets used in AI training.
- **Archival and Backup:** Suitable for long-term data retention and backups.

Block Storage

Block storage stores data in fixed-sized blocks and is typically used in scenarios where low-latency access and high performance are required.

Block Storage Examples:

- Amazon EBS (Elastic Block Store)
- Google Persistent Disks
- Azure Managed Disks

Advantages of Block storage:

- **Performance:** Provides high I/O performance, suitable for demanding applications.
- **Flexibility:** Can be attached to any instance and formatted with any file system.

Use Cases:

- **High-Performance Applications:** Suitable for applications such as databases and enterprise applications requiring fast data access.
- **Primary Storage:** Ideal for use as primary storage for virtual machines and containers running AI workloads.

File Storage

File storage manages data in a hierarchical structure, making it accessible through standard file system protocols.

Examples Of File Storage:

- Amazon EFS (Elastic File System)
- Google Filestore
- Azure Files

Advantages of File Storage:

- Simplicity: Provides a familiar file system interface.

- Shared Access: Supports shared access across multiple instances and users.
- Scalability: Automatically scales storage capacity as needed.

Use Cases:

- **Collaborative Workflows:** Ideal for applications that require file-level access and collaboration.
- **Shared Data Repositories:** Suitable for machine learning workflows involving multiple users and shared data access.

High-Performance Storage Options

High-performance storage solutions are essential for managing the large volumes of data and ensuring the rapid data access required by AI workloads, especially those involving generative models. This chapter explores the different types of high-performance storage solutions, their benefits, and how they can be effectively utilized in AI projects.

Types of High-Performance Storage Solutions

- **Solid-State Drives (SSDs)**
  SSDs are non-volatile storage devices that use flash memory to provide faster data access compared to traditional hard disk drives (HDDs).
  - ○ **Advantages:**

- **Speed:** Provides faster read and write speeds, reducing data access latency.
- **Reliability:** More resistant to physical shock and less prone to mechanical failure.
- **Energy Efficiency:** Consumes less power compared to HDDs.
  - **Use Cases:**
    - **Training Data Storage:** Suitable for storing datasets required for training AI models.
    - **Boot Drives:** Ideal for operating systems and software that require fast boot times.
  - **Example:**
    - Amazon EC2 Instances with Local NVMe SSDs Provides high IOPS and low latency for high-performance applications.

- **Non-Volatile Memory Express (NVMe) Storage**
  NVMe is a protocol designed specifically for SSDs to improve the speed and efficiency of data transfer.
  - **Advantages:**
    - **High Throughput:** Delivers higher throughput and lower latency compared to traditional storage protocols.
    - **Scalability:** Supports multiple queues for parallel data access, enhancing performance.
  - **Use Cases:**

- **Real-Time Analytics:** Suitable for applications requiring rapid data processing and analysis.
- **High-Performance Databases:** Ideal for database applications that demand high I/O performance.
  - **Example:**
    - **Amazon FSx for Lustre:** A high-performance file system optimized for fast processing of workloads, often paired with NVMe storage.

- **In-Memory Storage**

  In-memory storage uses RAM to store data, providing the fastest data access speeds.
  - **Advantages:**
    - **Ultra-Low Latency:** Offers the fastest read and write speeds by keeping data in memory.
    - **Performance:** Significantly improves application performance by reducing data access times.

  - **Use Cases:**
    - **AI Model Training:** Suitable for training deep learning models where data access speed is critical.
    - **Real-Time Applications:** Ideal for applications requiring immediate data access and processing.
  - **Example:**

- **Amazon ElastiCache:** Provides in-memory data storage and caching services, using Redis or Memcached.
- **Parallel File Systems**

  Parallel file systems are designed to provide high throughput by distributing data across multiple storage nodes.

  - **Advantages:**
    - **Scalability:** Easily scales to handle large volumes of data and high I/O demands.
    - **High Throughput**: Provides fast data access by leveraging multiple storage nodes.
  - **Use Cases:**
    - **High-Performance Computing (HPC):** Suitable for HPC applications requiring fast and scalable data access.
    - **Large-Scale AI Training:** Ideal for training large AI models with massive datasets.
  - **Example:**

    - **Amazon FSx for Lustre:** A parallel file system that provides high performance for processing large datasets.

Comparative Analysis of High-Performance Storage Solutions

- **Performance**

- o **NVMe Storage:** Offers even higher throughput and lower latency, ideal for real-time analytics and high-performance databases.
- o **In-Memory Storage:** Delivers the fastest data access speeds, essential for real-time applications and AI model training.
- o **Parallel File Systems:** Provide high throughput and scalability, suitable for HPC and large-scale AI training.

- **Cost Efficiency**
  - o **SSDs:** Generally more expensive than HDDs but offer better performance.
  - o **NVMe Storage:** Higher cost compared to standard SSDs but justified by the performance gains.
  - o **In-Memory Storage:** Can be expensive due to the cost of RAM, but offers unparalleled speed.
  - o **Parallel File Systems:** Cost varies based on the scale and configuration, suitable for high-demand applications.

- **Scalability**
  - o **SSDs:** Easily scalable, suitable for expanding storage capacity as needed.
  - o **NVMe Storage:** Scales well with increasing I/O demands.
  - o **In-Memory Storage:** Limited by the amount of available RAM, but can be scaled within those constraints.
  - o **Parallel File Systems:** Highly scalable, designed to handle large volumes of data and high I/O workloads.

Best Practices for Optimizing High-Performance Storage

To maximize the efficiency and effectiveness of high-performance storage solutions, consider the following best practices:

- **Profile Workloads:** Analyze your AI workloads to determine the most suitable storage solutions based on performance requirements.
- **Optimize Data Layout:** Organize data to minimize access times and improve performance.
- **Implement Caching:** Use caching strategies to reduce the need for repeated data access from slower storage tiers.
- **Monitor Performance:** Continuously monitor storage performance metrics to identify and address bottlenecks.
- **Balance Cost and Performance:** Select storage solutions that offer the best balance between cost and performance for your specific use cases.

Use Case: Training a Generative AI Model

Let's consider an example of training a generative AI model using high-performance storage solutions:

- **Data Ingestion:** Store raw data in Amazon S3 (object storage) for scalability and durability.
- **Data Preprocessing:** Use Amazon EFS (file storage) to share and preprocess data across multiple instances.

- **High-Performance Storage for Training:** Utilize Amazon FSx for Lustre (parallel file system) to provide high throughput and scalability for training instances.
- **In-Memory Caching:** Implement Amazon ElastiCache (in-memory storage) to cache frequently accessed data, reducing latency during training.
- **Model Storage and Access:** Store trained models in Amazon S3 and use Amazon CloudFront (CDN) to distribute model inference results globally with low latency

Inference

High-performance storage solutions are crucial for managing the large volumes of data and ensuring the rapid data access required by AI workloads. By understanding the characteristics and benefits of different high-performance storage options, you can select the most appropriate solutions for your generative AI projects. Implementing best practices for storage optimization will ensure optimal performance, scalability, and cost-efficiency.

Data Management and Storage Strategies

Effective data management and storage strategies are crucial for optimizing AI workflows. Proper data handling ensures the efficient processing of large datasets, improves performance, and helps manage costs. This chapter explores various data management and storage strategies tailored for AI workloads.

Data Lifecycle Management

Data Ingestion

Data ingestion is the process of collecting and importing data for immediate use or storage in a database.

Strategies:

- **Automated Ingestion Pipelines**: Implement automated pipelines to continuously gather data from various sources.
- **Batch vs. Stream Processing**: Choose between batch processing for bulk data and stream processing for real-time data.

Tools:

- **Apache Kafka:** For real-time data streaming.
- **AWS Glue:** For creating ETL (Extract, Transform, Load) jobs.

Data Preprocessing

Data preprocessing involves cleaning, transforming, and organizing data before it is used in AI models.

Strategies:

- **Data Cleaning**: Remove duplicates, handle missing values, and correct errors.
- **Normalization and Scaling**: Transform data into a standard format for consistency.

Tools:

- **Pandas**: A Python library for data manipulation and analysis.
- **Scikit-learn**: For data preprocessing and feature engineering.

Data Storage

Choosing the right storage solution is essential for managing large datasets efficiently.

Strategies:

- **Hierarchical Storage Management (HSM):** Use different storage tiers based on data access frequency.
- **Data Partitioning:** Divide large datasets into manageable parts to improve query performance.

Tools:

- **Amazon S3:** For scalable object storage.
- **Amazon Redshift:** For data warehousing and analytics.

High-Performance Storage Solutions

Object Storage:

Object storage is ideal for handling large amounts of unstructured data.

Advantages:

- **Scalability:** Easily scales to store vast amounts of data.
- **Durability:** High durability through data replication across multiple locations.

Example:

- **Amazon S3:** Provides object storage with high durability and scalability.

Block Storage:

Block storage offers high performance and low-latency access.

Advantages:

- **High I/O Performance:** Suitable for demanding applications.
- **Flexibility:** Can be attached to any instance and formatted with any file system.

Example:

- **Amazon EBS**: Elastic Block Store provides high I/O performance for EC2 instances.

File Storage:

File storage provides a familiar file system interface for managing data.
Advantages:
- **Shared Access:** Supports shared access across multiple instances.
- **Scalability:** Automatically scales storage capacity as needed.

Example:
- **Amazon EFS:** Elastic File System provides scalable file storage for multiple instances.

Data Governance and Security

Data Governance:

Data governance ensures data quality, consistency, and security across the organization.

Strategies:

- **Data Policies**: Establish policies for data access, usage, and retention.
- **Data Catalogs**: Maintain a catalog of data assets to facilitate discovery and management.

Tools:

- **AWS Glue Data Catalog**: Provides a central repository for storing and managing metadata.

Data Security:

Implementing robust security measures is crucial for protecting data.

Strategies:

- **Encryption**: Encrypt data at rest and in transit to protect it from unauthorized access.
- **Access Controls**: Use Identity and Access Management (IAM) to control who can access data.

Tools:

- **AWS KMS (Key Management Service)**: Manages encryption keys for data security.
- **AWS IAM**: Provides fine-grained access control to AWS resources.

Data Analytics and Visualization

Data Analytics:

Analyzing data helps derive insights and make informed decisions.

Strategies:

- **Batch Analytics**: Analyze large datasets in batches for comprehensive insights.
- **Real-Time Analytics**: Analyze data in real-time for immediate insights.

Tools:

- **Amazon Redshift**: For data warehousing and complex queries.
- **Amazon Athena**: For querying data in S3 using standard SQL.

Data Visualization:

Visualizing data helps communicate insights effectively.

Strategies:

- **Dashboards**: Create interactive dashboards to visualize key metrics and trends.
- **Charts and Graphs**: Use various chart types to represent data visually.

Tools:

- **Amazon QuickSight**: A business intelligence service for creating interactive dashboards.
- **Tableau**: A popular data visualization tool.

Best Practices for Data Management and Storage

To maximize the efficiency and effectiveness of your data management and storage strategies, consider the following best practices:

- **Data Organization:** Organize data logically to facilitate efficient access and management.
- **Data Lifecycle Policies:** Implement data lifecycle policies to move data between different storage classes based on access patterns and retention requirements.
- **Regular Backups:** Ensure regular backups to protect against data loss.
- **Data Quality Checks:** Perform regular data quality checks to maintain data integrity.
- **Compliance:** Ensure compliance with regulatory requirements such as GDPR, HIPAA, and CCPA.

Use Case: End-to-End AI Workflow

Let's consider an example of an end-to-end AI workflow utilizing data management and storage strategies:

- **Data Ingestion:** Collect raw data (e.g., images, text) using AWS Glue for ETL jobs and store it in Amazon S3 (object storage).
- **Data Preprocessing:** Clean, normalize, and partition data using Pandas and Scikit-learn.
- **Data Storage:** Use Amazon EFS (file storage) to share preprocessed data across multiple instances for collaborative work.

- **Model Training:** Leverage Amazon EBS (block storage) for high-performance storage during model training.
- **Data Governance and Security:** Use AWS Glue Data Catalog for metadata management and AWS KMS for data encryption.
- **Data Analytics and Visualization:** Analyze data with Amazon Redshift and visualize insights with Amazon QuickSight.

Inference

Effective data management and storage strategies are essential for optimizing AI workflows. By understanding the various data management techniques and storage solutions, you can ensure efficient data handling, improved performance, and cost-effectiveness. Implementing best practices for data organization, security, and analytics will help you maximize the value of your data and drive successful AI projects.

Integrating Storage with Compute Resources

Integrating storage solutions with compute resources is crucial for the efficient handling of AI workloads. Proper integration ensures fast data access, smooth data flow, and optimized performance. This chapter discusses strategies and best practices for integrating various storage solutions with compute resources in cloud environments.

Understanding Storage and Compute Resources

Storage Solutions:

- **Object Storage:** Ideal for storing large amounts of unstructured data. Example: Amazon S3.
- **Block Storage:** Provides high-performance, low-latency access. Example: Amazon EBS.
- **File Storage:** Manages data in a hierarchical structure with shared access. Example: Amazon EFS.

Compute Resources:

- **Virtual Machines (VMs):** Provide a flexible and scalable environment for various tasks.
- **Graphics Processing Units (GPUs):** Specialized processors designed for parallel computations, ideal for training AI models.
- **Tensor Processing Units (TPUs):** Custom-developed by Google to accelerate machine learning workloads.
- **Field-Programmable Gate Arrays (FPGAs):** Configurable integrated circuits offering custom performance for specific applications.

Integration Strategies

Direct Integration:

Direct integration involves connecting storage solutions directly to compute resources. This approach is suitable for workloads requiring fast and reliable data access.

Example:

- **Amazon EC2 with EBS:** Attach Amazon EBS volumes to EC2 instances for high-performance block storage.

Network File Systems:

Network file systems enable multiple compute instances to access shared storage over a network. This approach is ideal for collaborative AI workloads.

Example:

- **Amazon EFS**: Provides scalable file storage that can be mounted on multiple EC2 instances simultaneously.

Object Storage Access:

Object storage can be accessed by compute resources using APIs. This approach is suitable for storing and retrieving large datasets in a scalable manner.

Example:

- **Amazon S3 with EC2**: Use the AWS SDK to access data stored in Amazon S3 from EC2 instances.

Best Practices for Integration

Optimizing Data Flow:

Ensure efficient data flow between storage and compute resources to minimize latency and improve performance.

Strategies:

- **Data Locality**: Store data close to the compute resources that process it.
- **Parallel Data Access**: Use parallel data access methods to speed up data transfer.

Tools:

- **Amazon Data Pipeline**: Automate the movement and transformation of data.

Security and Compliance:

Implement robust security measures to protect data and ensure compliance with regulatory requirements

Strategies:

- **Encryption**: Encrypt data at rest and in transit.
- **Access Controls**: Use IAM policies to control access to storage and compute resources.

Tools:

- **AWS KMS**: Manage encryption keys.
- **AWS IAM**: Implement fine-grained access control.

Monitoring and Optimization:

Continuously monitor the performance of integrated storage and compute resources and optimize configurations as needed.

Strategies:

- **Performance Metrics**: Monitor I/O performance, latency, and throughput.
- **Cost Management**: Use cost management tools to optimize resource usage and reduce expenses.

Tools:

- **Amazon CloudWatch**: Monitor resource performance and set up alarms.
- **AWS Cost Explorer**: Analyze and manage AWS costs and usage.

Use Case: Training a Generative AI Model

Let's consider an example of training a generative AI model with integrated storage and compute resources:

- **Data Ingestion and Storage:** Use Amazon S3 to store raw data and AWS Glue to create ETL jobs for preprocessing.
- **High-Performance Storage for Training:** Use Amazon FSx for Lustre for high-throughput data access during model training.
- **Compute Resources:** Leverage Amazon EC2 instances with attached EBS volumes and GPUs for training the model.
- **Model Storage and Access:** Store the trained model in Amazon S3 and use Amazon CloudFront to distribute inference results globally.
- **Monitoring and Optimization:** Use Amazon CloudWatch to monitor performance and AWS Cost Explorer to manage costs.

Inference

Integrating storage solutions with compute resources is essential for optimizing AI workloads. By following best practices for data flow optimization, security, and monitoring, you can ensure efficient and high-performance data handling. Proper integration helps manage large datasets effectively and supports the demanding requirements of generative AI models.

CHAPTER 5
Networking and Data Transfer

Networking and data transfer are critical components of cloud infrastructure for AI workloads. Efficient networking ensures fast data movement, low latency, and secure communication between various resources. This chapter explores networking concepts, data transfer strategies, and best practices for optimizing networking performance in AI workloads.

When it comes to AI, networking and data transfer require a robust infrastructure capable of handling large volumes of data with high speed and low latency, typically utilizing dedicated high-bandwidth connections, optimized network architectures like Clos fabrics, and features like RDMA to efficiently move data between GPUs for parallel processing, ensuring smooth training and inference of AI models across distributed computing environments; this often involves specialized solutions designed specifically for AI workloads to manage the unique demands of data intensive operations

Key Networking Concepts

Virtual Private Cloud (VPC)

A Virtual Private Cloud (VPC) is a private, isolated section of the cloud where you can launch resources within a virtual network that you define.

- **Features:**
    - ○ **Isolation**: Provides network isolation for enhanced security.
    - ○ **Customization**: Allows customization of network configurations such as subnets, route tables, and gateways.
- **Example:**
    - ○ **Amazon VPC**: Allows you to define a virtual network in the AWS cloud.

Subnets

Subnets are subdivisions of a VPC that allow you to group and isolate resources based on security and operational requirements.

- **Features:**
    - ○ **Network Segmentation:** Enables segmentation of network traffic for security and performance.
    - ○ **Custom Routing:** Allows custom routing policies for traffic management.
- **Example:**
    - ○ **Public and Private Subnets:** Use public subnets for internet-facing resources and private subnets for internal resources.

Gateways and Endpoints

Gateways and endpoints provide connectivity between your VPC and other networks or services.

- **Features:**
  - **Internet Gateway**: Provides internet access to resources in a VPC.
  - **NAT Gateway**: Allows instances in a private subnet to connect to the internet without exposing them to inbound traffic.
  - **VPC Endpoints**: Provide private connectivity to AWS services without traversing the internet.
- **Example:**
  - **AWS VPC Endpoints**: Enable private access to AWS services like S3 and DynamoDB.

Load Balancing

Load balancing distributes incoming traffic across multiple resources to ensure high availability and reliability.

- **Features:**

  - **Traffic Distribution**: Distributes traffic evenly across multiple instances.

  - **Health Checks**: Monitors the health of instances and routes traffic only to healthy instances.

- **Example:**

    - o **Amazon Elastic Load Balancer (ELB)**: Distributes incoming application traffic across multiple EC2 instances.

Data Transfer Strategies

Data Transfer Services

Data transfer services facilitate the movement of large datasets into and out of the cloud.

- **Examples:**

    - o **AWS DataSync**: Automates the transfer of data between on-premises storage and AWS storage services.

    - o **AWS Snowball**: Physically transfers large amounts of data using a secure appliance.

Direct Data Transfer

Direct data transfer involves uploading data directly to cloud storage services using APIs or web interfaces.

- **Examples:**
    - o **Amazon S3 Transfer Acceleration:** Speeds up uploads to S3 by using Amazon CloudFront's globally distributed edge locations.

Hybrid Data Transfer

Hybrid data transfer combines on-premises storage with cloud storage to enable seamless data movement and access.

- **Examples:**
  - **AWS Storage Gateway:** Connects on-premises environments with AWS cloud storage.

Best Practices for Networking and Data Transfer

Optimizing Network Performance

Ensure optimal network performance by minimizing latency, maximizing throughput, and reducing network congestion.

Strategies:

- **Use Elastic Load Balancing**: Distribute traffic across multiple instances to balance load and improve performance.

- **Enable VPC Endpoints**: Reduce latency by establishing private connections to AWS services.

- **Implement Data Compression**: Compress data to reduce the amount of data being transferred.

Tools:

- **Amazon CloudFront**: A CDN that speeds up the distribution of your static and dynamic web content.

Ensuring Security

Implement robust security measures to protect data in transit and ensure compliance with regulatory requirements.

Strategies:
- **Encrypt Data in Transit:** Use protocols like TLS/SSL to encrypt data during transfer.
- **Use Private Networking:** Utilize VPCs, subnets, and private IP addressing to keep data secure within the network.
- **Implement Firewalls and Security Groups:** Control inbound and outbound traffic to resources using security groups and network ACLs.

Tools:
- **AWS Key Management Service (KMS):** Manage encryption keys.
- **AWS Security Groups:** Act as virtual firewalls for your instances.

Monitoring and Troubleshooting

Continuously monitor network performance and troubleshoot issues to maintain optimal operation.

Strategies:

- **Monitor Network Traffic**: Use monitoring tools to track network traffic patterns and identify bottlenecks.
- **Set Up Alerts**: Configure alerts for unusual network activity or performance degradation.

Tools:

- **Amazon CloudWatch**: Monitor and collect log data from AWS resources.
- **AWS VPC Flow Logs**: Capture information about the IP traffic going to and from network interfaces in your VPC.

Use Case: Data Transfer for AI Model Training

Let's consider an example of transferring data for AI model training using various networking and data transfer strategies:

- **Data Ingestion:** Use AWS DataSync to transfer large datasets from on-premises storage to Amazon S3.
- **Network Configuration:** Set up a secure Amazon VPC with private and public subnets, and use VPC endpoints for private access to S3.
- **Optimizing Data Transfer:** Enable Amazon S3 Transfer Acceleration to speed up data uploads.
- **Security Measures:** Encrypt data in transit using TLS/SSL and control access with security groups.
- **Monitoring and Optimization:** Use Amazon CloudWatch to monitor network performance and set up alerts for any anomalies.

Inference:

Efficient networking and data transfer are critical for optimizing AI workloads in the cloud. By understanding key networking concepts, data transfer strategies, and best practices, you can ensure fast, secure, and reliable data movement. Proper integration of these elements helps manage large datasets effectively and supports the demanding requirements of generative AI models.

Importance of Efficient Networking

Efficient networking is a cornerstone of cloud infrastructure for AI workloads. It ensures that data is transferred quickly and securely between different components of an AI system. This chapter discusses the critical role of efficient networking in AI, the benefits it offers, and best practices to optimize network performance.

Why Efficient Networking Matters

1. **Data Transfer Speed**

   AI workloads, especially those involving large datasets, require fast data transfer to minimize latency and improve processing times.
   - **Benefits:**
     - **Reduced Training Time**: Faster data transfer speeds reduce the time required to train AI models.
     - **Real-Time Processing**: Enables real-time data processing and analytics, essential for applications like autonomous vehicles and live video analysis.

2. Low Latency

Low latency is crucial for applications that require immediate response times, such as real-time inference and interactive AI systems.

- o **Benefits:**
    - **Improved User Experience:** Low latency ensures quick responses, enhancing user experience.
    - **Effective Real-Time Applications:** Critical for applications like online gaming, virtual reality, and financial trading systems.

3. High Throughput

High throughput allows the network to handle large volumes of data efficiently, which is essential for AI workloads that involve massive data transfers.

- o **Benefits:**
    - **Scalability:** Supports scalable AI workloads by efficiently handling high data transfer rates.
    - **Performance:** Maintains high performance even under heavy data loads.

4. Network Reliability

Reliable networking ensures consistent and uninterrupted data transfer, which is vital for the stability and performance of AI systems.

- o **Benefits:**

- **Business Continuity:** Minimizes downtime and ensures continuous operation of critical AI applications.
- **Data Integrity:** Reduces the risk of data loss or corruption during transfer.

Networking Components for AI Workloads

1. **Virtual Private Cloud (VPC)**

   A VPC provides a secure and isolated network environment in the cloud, allowing you to launch resources in a virtual network that you define.
   - **Features:**
     - **Isolation:** Enhances security by isolating network traffic.
     - **Customization:** Offers customizable network configurations such as subnets, route tables, and gateways.

2. **Elastic Load Balancing**

   Elastic Load Balancing distributes incoming traffic across multiple resources to ensure high availability and reliability.
   - **Features:**
     - **Traffic Distribution:** Balances load to prevent any single instance from becoming a bottleneck.
     - **Health Checks:** Routes traffic only to healthy instances, ensuring reliability.

3. **Content Delivery Networks (CDN)**

   CDNs distribute content geographically to reduce latency and improve access speed for end-users.
   - **Features:**

- **Edge Locations:** Serve content from the nearest edge location to the user, reducing latency.
- **Scalability:** Easily scale to handle large volumes of traffic.

Best Practices for Achieving Efficient Networking

1. Optimize Data Flow

Ensuring efficient data flow between storage and compute resources minimizes latency and maximizes throughput.

- **Strategies:**
  - **Data Locality**: Store data close to compute resources to minimize data transfer times.
  - **Parallel Data Access**: Use parallel data access methods to speed up data transfer.

2. Implement Security Measures

Secure your network to protect data in transit and comply with regulatory requirements.

- **Strategies:**
  - **Encryption:** Encrypt data at rest and in transit to protect it from unauthorized access.
  - **Access Controls:** Use IAM policies to control access to network resources.

Monitor and Troubleshoot Network Performance

Continuously monitor network performance to identify and address issues promptly.

- **Strategies:**
  - ○ **Performance Metrics**: Track metrics such as latency, throughput, and packet loss.
  - ○ **Set Up Alerts**: Configure alerts for unusual network activity or performance degradation.

Use Case: Real-Time AI Inference

Let's consider an example of real-time AI inference, highlighting the importance of efficient networking:

- **Network Configuration**: Set up a secure Amazon VPC with private and public subnets, and use VPC endpoints for private access to AWS services.
- **Data Transfer**: Use AWS DataSync to transfer data quickly between on-premises storage and AWS cloud storage.
- **Load Balancing**: Implement Amazon ELB to distribute incoming inference requests across multiple EC2 instances.
- **Content Delivery**: Use Amazon CloudFront (CDN) to distribute inference results globally with low latency.
- **Security Measures**: Encrypt data in transit using TLS/SSL and control access with security groups.
- **Monitoring and Optimization**: Use Amazon CloudWatch to monitor network performance and set up alerts for any anomalies.

Inference:

Efficient networking is crucial for optimizing AI workloads in the cloud. By ensuring fast data transfer, low latency, high throughput, and network reliability, you can enhance the performance and scalability of AI applications. Implementing best practices for data flow optimization, security, and monitoring will help you achieve efficient networking and drive successful AI projects.

High-Speed Networking Technologies

High-speed networking technologies are essential for optimizing the performance of AI workloads, especially those involving large datasets and real-time processing. This chapter discusses key high-speed networking technologies, their advantages, use cases, and best practices for leveraging them in cloud environments.

Key High-Speed Networking Technologies

infrastructure in a safe, consistent, and repeatable way by defining resource configurations that you can version, reuse, and share.

1. **InfiniBand**

   InfiniBand is a high-speed, low-latency networking technology commonly used in high-performance computing (HPC) environments.

- o **Advantages:**

  - **Low Latency**: Offers extremely low latency, making it ideal for latency-sensitive applications.

  - **High Throughput**: Provides high data transfer rates, supporting fast data movement between nodes.

  - **Scalability**: Easily scales to accommodate large HPC clusters and AI workloads.

- o **Use Cases:**

  - **HPC Clusters:** Suitable for connecting nodes in HPC clusters for scientific computing, simulations, and large-scale AI training.

  - **Real-Time Analytics:** Ideal for applications requiring real-time data processing and analytics.

- o **Example:**

  - **AWS EC2 Instances with Elastic Fabric Adapter (EFA):** EFA provides low-latency networking for EC2 instances, leveraging InfiniBand technology.

2. 100 Gbps Ethernet

100 Gbps Ethernet provides high-speed networking for data centers, enabling fast and efficient data transfer.

- o **Advantages:**

    - **High Bandwidth:** Delivers high bandwidth for data-intensive applications.

    - **Reduced Congestion:** Minimizes network congestion, ensuring smooth data flow.

    - **Interoperability:** Compatible with existing Ethernet infrastructure.

- o **Use Cases:**

    - **Data Centers:** Suitable for connecting servers and storage devices in data centers.

    - **AI Training:** Ideal for transferring large datasets during AI model training.

- o **Example:**

    - **Google Cloud Platform:** Offers 100 Gbps Ethernet connectivity for high-performance computing and AI workloads.

3. **Software-Defined Networking (SDN)**

SDN is an approach to networking that uses software-based controllers to manage network resources and traffic.

- o **Advantages:**

  - **Centralized Control:** Provides centralized control of network resources, allowing for dynamic and automated management.

  - **Flexibility:** Enables easy reconfiguration of network settings to adapt to changing requirements.

  - **Optimized Traffic Flow:** Enhances traffic flow optimization through programmable network policies.

- o **Use Cases:**

  - **Cloud Environments:** Suitable for managing network resources in cloud environments, providing flexibility and scalability.

  - **AI and IoT Applications:** Ideal for applications requiring dynamic network configurations and low-latency communication.

- o **Example:**

- **Microsoft Azure Virtual Network:** Provides SDN capabilities for managing and optimizing network resources in Azure.

4. **Edge Computing**

Edge computing involves processing data at or near the source of data generation, reducing latency and bandwidth usage.

- ○ **Advantages:**

  - **Low Latency:** Reduces latency by processing data closer to the source.

  - **Bandwidth Optimization:** Minimizes the need to transfer large amounts of data to centralized data centers.

  - **Real-Time Processing:** Enables real-time data processing and decision-making.

- ○ **Use Cases:**

  - **IoT Devices:** Suitable for processing data generated by IoT devices at the edge.

  - **Autonomous Systems:** Ideal for applications like autonomous vehicles and drones that require immediate data processing.

- Example:

  - **AWS Greengrass:** Extends AWS capabilities to edge devices, enabling local data processing and machine learning inference.

Comparative Analysis of High-Speed Networking Technologies

Performance

- **InfiniBand**: Provides the lowest latency and highest throughput, suitable for HPC and real-time analytics.

- **100 Gbps Ethernet**: Offers high bandwidth for data-intensive applications, with reduced network congestion.

- **SDN**: Enhances flexibility and control over network resources, optimizing traffic flow.

- **Edge Computing:** Reduces latency and bandwidth usage by processing data closer to the source.

Cost Efficiency

- **InfiniBand:** Higher cost due to specialized hardware, but justified by performance gains in HPC and AI training.

- **100 Gbps Ethernet:** Cost-effective for upgrading existing Ethernet infrastructure to higher speeds.

- **SDN:** Cost savings through centralized management and automation of network resources.

- **Edge Computing:** Cost-effective for reducing bandwidth usage and latency, especially in IoT applications.

Scalability

- **InfiniBand:** Scales well for large HPC clusters and AI workloads.

- **100 Gbps Ethernet:** Easily scales within data centers, supporting high-performance computing.

- **SDN:** Provides scalable network management through software-based controllers.

- **Edge Computing:** Scales effectively by distributing processing power across edge devices.

Best Practices for Leveraging High-Speed Networking Technologies

To maximize the benefits of high-speed networking technologies, consider the following best practices:

1. **Analyze Workloads**: Profile your AI workloads to determine the most suitable networking technology based on performance requirements.

2. **Optimize Network Configuration**: Configure network settings to minimize latency, maximize throughput, and reduce congestion.

3. **Implement Security Measures**: Ensure robust security protocols to protect data in transit and comply with regulatory requirements.

4. **Monitor Performance**: Continuously monitor network performance metrics to identify and address bottlenecks.

5. **Leverage Hybrid Approaches**: Combine multiple networking technologies to meet diverse workload requirements and optimize performance.

Use Case: High-Performance AI Training

Let's consider an example of high-performance AI training using high-speed networking technologies:

1. **Network Setup**: Configure a VPC with low-latency networking using InfiniBand technology for connecting compute nodes.

2. **Data Transfer**: Use 100 Gbps Ethernet to transfer large datasets from storage to compute resources quickly.

3. **Traffic Management**: Implement SDN to dynamically manage network traffic and optimize data flow.

4. **Edge Processing**: Utilize edge computing to preprocess data at the source, reducing the amount of data transferred to the cloud.

5. **Security Measures**: Encrypt data in transit and control access with security groups and network ACLs.

6. **Monitoring and Optimization**: Use network monitoring tools to track performance and make adjustments as needed.

Inference

High-speed networking technologies are essential for optimizing AI workloads in cloud environments. By leveraging technologies like InfiniBand, 100 Gbps Ethernet, SDN, and edge computing, you can ensure fast, secure, and reliable data transfer. Implementing best practices for network configuration, security, and performance monitoring will help you achieve efficient networking and drive successful AI projects.

Data Transfer Optimization

Optimizing data transfer is crucial for enhancing the performance of AI workloads, particularly those involving large datasets and real-time processing. This chapter discusses key strategies and best practices for optimizing data transfer in cloud environments to achieve high throughput, low latency, and cost efficiency.

Importance of Data Transfer Optimization

1. Reduced Latency

Minimizing the time it takes for data to move between different components of an AI system.

Benefits:

- **Faster Training and Inference:** Reduces the time required to train and deploy AI models.
- **Improved User Experience:** Ensures quick responses for real-time applications.

2. Increased Throughput

Maximizing the amount of data that can be transferred in a given period.

Benefits:

- **Handling Large Datasets:** Efficiently processes massive amounts of data.
- **Scalability:** Supports scalable AI workloads by accommodating high data transfer rates.

3. Cost Efficiency

Reducing the cost associated with data transfer.

Benefits:

- **Lower Operational Costs:** Minimizes the expenses related to moving data across networks.
- **Resource Optimization:** Ensures optimal use of available resources.

Key Strategies for Data Transfer Optimization

1. Data Compression

Compressing data before transfer to reduce its size and minimize the amount of data being transmitted.

Techniques:

- **Lossless Compression:** Reduces data size without losing any information. Suitable for critical data where accuracy is essential.
- **Lossy Compression:** Reduces data size by removing some information. Suitable for applications where slight data loss is acceptable.

Tools:

- **Gzip:** A widely used tool for data compression.
- **Snappy:** A fast data compression and decompression library.

2. Parallel Data Transfer

Transferring data in parallel streams to maximize throughput and reduce transfer time

Techniques:

- **Multipart Uploads:** Splits large files into smaller parts and uploads them in parallel.
- **Concurrent Connections:** Establishes multiple connections to transfer different parts of data simultaneously.

Tools:

- **AWS S3 Multipart Upload:** Supports multipart uploads to speed up data transfer to S3.
- **ParallelCluster:** AWS tool for managing HPC clusters and optimizing data transfer.

3. **Optimizing Network Configuration**

Configuring network settings to enhance data transfer performance.

Techniques:

- **Choosing Optimal Regions:** Selecting cloud regions closer to data sources to minimize latency.
- **Using Direct Connections:** Establishing direct connections to cloud services to improve data transfer speed.

Tools:

- **AWS Direct Connect:** Provides a dedicated network connection to AWS.
- **Azure ExpressRoute:** Offers private connections between Azure data centers and on-premises infrastructure.

4. Caching Strategies

Implementing caching mechanisms to store frequently accessed data closer to compute resources.

Techniques:

- **Edge Caching:** Caching data at edge locations to reduce latency for global users.
- **In-Memory Caching:** Storing data in memory for fast access.

Tools:

- **Amazon CloudFront:** A CDN that caches content at edge locations.
- **Amazon ElastiCache:** Provides in-memory caching using Redis or Memcached.

Best Practices for Data Transfer Optimization

Profile Data Transfer Needs

Analyze the specific data transfer requirements of your AI workloads to determine the most suitable optimization techniques.

Steps:

- **Identify Data Sources and Destinations:** Map out where data is coming from and where it needs to go.
- **Assess Data Transfer Patterns:** Evaluate the volume, frequency, and type of data transfers.

Leverage Data Transfer Services

Utilize specialized data transfer services to simplify and accelerate data movement.

Examples:

- **AWS DataSync:** Automates data transfers between on-premises storage and AWS.
- **Google Transfer Appliance:** Physically transfers large datasets to Google Cloud.

Implement Security Measures

Ensure that data transfers are secure to protect sensitive information and comply with regulatory requirements.

Techniques:

- **Encrypt Data in Transit:** Use TLS/SSL to encrypt data during transfer.
- **Access Controls:** Implement IAM policies to control access to data transfer services.

Monitor and Optimize

Continuously monitor data transfer performance and make adjustments as needed to optimize efficiency.

Tools:

- **Amazon CloudWatch:** Monitors data transfer metrics and performance.
- **Azure Monitor:** Provides insights into data transfer operations and network performance.

Use Case: High-Volume Data Transfer for AI Training

Let's consider an example of optimizing high-volume data transfer for AI model training:

1. **Data Compression:** Use Gzip to compress large datasets before transfer to Amazon S3.

2. **Parallel Uploads:** Implement S3 Multipart Upload to transfer data in parallel streams.

3. **Optimal Regions:** Choose AWS regions closest to data sources to reduce latency.

4. **Direct Connections:** Establish an AWS Direct Connect link for dedicated, high-speed data transfer.

5. **Edge Caching:** Utilize Amazon CloudFront to cache data at edge locations, reducing latency for global access.

6. **Monitoring:** Use Amazon CloudWatch to monitor data transfer performance and optimize configurations as needed.

Inference

Optimizing data transfer is essential for enhancing the performance and efficiency of AI workloads. By implementing strategies such as data compression, parallel data transfer, network optimization, and caching, you can achieve high throughput, low latency, and cost efficiency. Following best practices for profiling data transfer needs, leveraging specialized services, and continuous monitoring will help you optimize data transfer operations and drive successful AI projects.

CHAPTER 6
Networking Security For Generative AI

Generative AI security is a critical area of focus as organizations increasingly adopt these advanced technologies. Generative AI security is a multifaceted challenge that requires careful attention to data privacy, model integrity, ethical considerations, compliance, and continuous monitoring. By implementing robust security measures, fostering collaboration, and staying informed about the latest developments, organizations can leverage generative AI while ensuring security and ethical use.

Generative AI Networking Security

Understand Networking Security for Generative AI Workloads

Generative AI models often require significant computational resources and large datasets. Efficient network infrastructure is crucial to support these demanding workloads.

Key Networking Considerations:

- **High-Speed Networking:**

  - **100GbE and 400GbE:** Ensure high-bandwidth connectivity between compute nodes and storage systems.

  - **RDMA (Remote Direct Memory Access):** Optimize data transfer between nodes by bypassing the kernel and directly accessing memory.

- **Low-Latency Networking:**

  - **Infiniband:** A high-performance interconnect for cluster computing.

  - **TCP/IP Optimization:** Tune TCP parameters to reduce latency and improve throughput.

- **Network Security:**

116

- ○ **Firewall Rules:** Implement strict firewall rules to protect the network from unauthorized access.

- ○ **Intrusion Detection Systems (IDS):** Monitor network traffic for malicious activity.

- ○ **Intrusion Prevention Systems (IPS):** Block malicious traffic in real-time.

key points of Generative AI Security:

1. Data Privacy and Protection

Generative AI models often require large datasets for training, which can include sensitive information. Ensuring data privacy and protection is paramount to prevent unauthorized access and misuse.

Ensuring Data Privacy

When training generative AI models, it's crucial to use data anonymization techniques to protect sensitive information. This includes removing personally identifiable information (PII) and using synthetic data when possible

Best Practices:

- • **Data Anonymization:** Remove or mask PII from datasets.

- **Synthetic Data:** Use synthetic datasets to train models without exposing real user data.

- **Encrypt:** data both at rest and in transit to protect it from unauthorized access.

Implementing Access Controls

Restrict access to sensitive data and AI models to authorized personnel only. Use robust access control mechanisms to prevent unauthorized access.

Tools:

- **Role-Based Access Control (RBAC):** Assign roles and permissions based on job responsibilities.

- **Multi-Factor Authentication (MFA):** Add an extra layer of security to user authentication.

2. Model Security

Protecting the integrity of generative AI models is essential. This includes safeguarding against tampering, unauthorized access, and ensuring that the models are not compromised.

Protecting Model Integrity

Ensure that generative AI models are protected from tampering and unauthorized access. Implement measures to verify the integrity of models and prevent malicious modifications.

Best Practices:

- **Model Versioning:** Keep track of different versions of the model to detect any unauthorized changes.

- **Checksums and Hashing:** Use checksums and hashing techniques to verify model integrity.

3. Ethical Considerations

Generative AI can produce outputs that may be inappropriate or biased. It's important to implement measures to detect and mitigate these issues to ensure ethical use of the technology.

Detecting and Mitigating Bias

Generative AI models can inadvertently learn and replicate biases present in the training data. Implement measures to detect and mitigate these biases to ensure fair and ethical AI outputs.

Best Practices:

- **Bias Detection Tools**: Use tools to analyze model outputs for biases.

- **Diverse Training Data**: Ensure that training datasets are diverse and representative.

Monitoring for Inappropriate Content

Generative AI models can sometimes produce inappropriate or harmful content. Implement content moderation mechanisms to filter and review model outputs.

Tools:

- **Content Moderation APIs**: Use APIs to automatically detect and filter inappropriate content.

- **Human Review**: Incorporate human reviewers to oversee and validate model outputs.

4. Compliance and Governance

Organizations must adhere to regulatory requirements and establish governance frameworks to manage the risks associated with generative AI. This includes regular audits and compliance checks.

Adhering to Regulatory Requirements

Ensure that generative AI practices comply with relevant regulations and standards, such as GDPR, HIPAA, and CCPA.

Best Practices:

- **Regular Audits**: Conduct regular audits to ensure compliance with regulatory requirements.

- **Data Governance Policies**: Implement and enforce data governance policies.

Establishing Governance Frameworks

Develop governance frameworks to manage the risks associated with generative AI. This includes defining roles, responsibilities, and processes for AI governance.

Tools:

- **Governance Platforms**: Use platforms that support AI governance and compliance.

5. Continuous Monitoring and Updates

Regularly monitoring the performance of generative AI models and updating them to address new vulnerabilities and threats is crucial for maintaining security.

Monitoring Model Performance

Regularly monitor the performance of generative AI models to detect any anomalies or degradation in performance.

Best Practices:

- **Performance Metrics**: Track key performance metrics and set up alerts for deviations.

- **Regular Evaluations**: Periodically evaluate model performance against benchmarks.

Updating Models and Security Protocols

Keep AI models and security protocols updated to address new vulnerabilities and threats.

Tools:

- **Automated Updates**: Use automated tools to apply updates and patches.

- **Model Retraining**: Regularly retrain models with updated data to maintain accuracy and relevance.

6. Collaboration and Knowledge Sharing

Fostering collaboration between AI experts and cybersecurity teams can help develop comprehensive security strategies and share best practices.

Fostering Interdisciplinary Collaboration

Encourage collaboration between AI experts, cybersecurity professionals, and other stakeholders to develop comprehensive security strategies.
Best Practices:

- **Interdisciplinary Teams**: Form teams with diverse expertise to address security challenges.

- **Knowledge Sharing**: Facilitate knowledge sharing through workshops, training sessions, and documentation.

Participating in Industry Initiatives

Engage with industry initiatives and communities focused on AI security to stay informed about the latest developments and best practices.

Examples:

- **AI Security Conferences**: Attend conferences and workshops on AI security.

- **Industry Working Groups**: Participate in working groups and forums dedicated to AI security.

Security Best Practices for Generative AI

Security is paramount when working with sensitive data and AI models. Here are some key security considerations:

- **Data Security:**
  - ○ **Encryption:** Encrypt data both at rest and in transit.
  - ○ **Access Controls:** Implement role-based access control to limit access to sensitive data.

- Data Loss Prevention (DLP): Prevent unauthorized data leakage.
- **Model Security:**
  - **Model Poisoning:** Protect models from malicious inputs that could degrade performance.
  - **Model Intellectual Property:** Secure model architectures and weights to prevent theft.
  - **Model Privacy:** Ensure that models do not inadvertently leak sensitive information.
- **Infrastructure Security:**
  - **Patch Management:** Keep all systems and software up-to-date with the latest security patches.
  - **Network Segmentation:** Isolate sensitive components of the infrastructure.
  - **Regular Security Audits:** Conduct regular security audits to identify and address vulnerabilities.
- **AI-Specific Security Threats:**
  - **Adversarial Attacks:** Defend against attacks that manipulate input data to deceive AI models.
  - **Model Extraction Attacks:** Protect models from being stolen or reverse-engineered.
  - **Model Inversion Attacks:** Prevent attackers from reconstructing training data from model outputs.

Additional Considerations:

- **Compliance and Regulations:** Adhere to relevant data privacy regulations (e.g., GDPR, CCPA, HIPAA).

- **Disaster Recovery and Business Continuity:** Implement robust disaster recovery and business continuity plans to minimize downtime.

- **Monitoring and Logging:** Monitor system and network performance, and log security events for analysis and incident response.

By following these guidelines, you can build a secure and efficient network infrastructure to support your generative AI workloads.

Adversarial Attacks on Generative AI Models

Adversarial attacks exploit vulnerabilities in AI models by introducing carefully crafted inputs that can mislead the model. These attacks can compromise the integrity and reliability of AI systems, particularly those in critical applications like autonomous vehicles or medical diagnosis.

Types of Adversarial Attacks:

1. **Fast Gradient Sign Method (FGSM):** This method adds a small perturbation to the input data, causing the model to misclassify it.
2. **Projected Gradient Descent (PGD):** A more sophisticated attack that iteratively improves the perturbation to maximize the model's misclassification.

3. **Carlini-Wagner (CW) Attack:** A powerful attack that finds adversarial examples that are imperceptible to humans but can significantly degrade model performance.

Defense Strategies:

1. **Adversarial Training:** Train models on a dataset that includes adversarial examples to improve their robustness.
2. **Defensive Distillation:** Distill a smaller, more robust model from a larger, more complex one.
3. **Input Transformations:** Apply random noise or other transformations to the input data to make it more resistant to adversarial attacks.
4. **Feature Squeezing:** Reduce the dimensionality of the input data to make it less susceptible to attacks.
5. **Detection-Based Defenses:** Use techniques like anomaly detection to identify and mitigate adversarial attacks.

Real-world Implications:

- **Autonomous Vehicles:** Adversarial attacks could trick self-driving cars into misinterpreting road signs or traffic signals.
- **Facial Recognition:** Adversarial attacks could bypass facial recognition systems, leading to security breaches.
- **Medical Diagnosis:** Adversarial attacks could mislead AI-powered medical diagnosis systems, resulting in incorrect diagnoses.

Additional Considerations:

- **Regular Security Audits:** Conduct regular security audits to identify and address vulnerabilities.
- **Stay Updated:** Keep up-to-date with the latest research on adversarial attacks and defense techniques.
- **Collaboration:** Work with the broader AI community to share knowledge and best practices.

By understanding the nature of adversarial attacks and implementing effective defense strategies, we can build more robust and resilient generative AI systems.

Data Privacy and Security in Generative AI

As generative AI models become increasingly sophisticated, so too do the privacy and security challenges associated with handling large datasets.

Key Considerations:

1. **Data Privacy Regulations:**
   - **GDPR:** The General Data Protection Regulation imposes strict rules on how personal data is collected, processed, and stored.
   - **CCPA:** The California Consumer Privacy Act grants consumers rights over their personal data.
   - **HIPAA:** The Health Insurance Portability and Accountability Act regulates the use and disclosure of health information.
2. **Data Security:**

- o **Encryption:** Encrypt data both at rest and in transit to protect it from unauthorized access.
- o **Access Controls:** Implement strong access controls to limit access to sensitive data.
- o **Regular Security Audits:** Conduct regular security audits to identify and address vulnerabilities.
- o **Incident Response Plan:** Have a plan in place to respond to data breaches and other security incidents.

3. **Model Privacy:**
   - o **Differential Privacy:** Add noise to data to protect individual privacy while preserving statistical properties.
   - o **Federated Learning:** Train models on decentralized data without sharing raw data.

4. **Ethical Considerations:**
   - o **Bias and Fairness:** Ensure that AI models are fair and unbiased.
   - o **Transparency:** Make AI models and their decision-making processes transparent.
   - o **Accountability:** Hold developers and organizations accountable for the ethical implications of AI.

Specific Challenges in Generative AI:

- **Data Leakage:** Sensitive data could be inadvertently leaked through model outputs or training data.
- **Model Inversion Attacks:** Attackers could reconstruct training data from model outputs.

- **Adversarial Attacks:** Malicious actors could manipulate input data to deceive AI models.

Best Practices:

- **Data Minimization:** Collect and store only the necessary data.
- **Purpose Limitation:** Use data only for its intended purpose.
- **Data Retention:** Implement data retention policies to delete unnecessary data.
- **Regular Security Training:** Train employees on security best practices.
- **Third-Party Risk Management:** Carefully assess and manage risks associated with third-party vendors.

By understanding and addressing these challenges, organizations can build and deploy generative AI models responsibly and ethically.

Inference

Generative AI security is a multifaceted challenge that requires careful attention to data privacy, model integrity, ethical considerations, compliance, and continuous monitoring. By implementing robust security measures, fostering collaboration, and staying informed about the latest developments, organizations can leverage generative AI while ensuring security and ethical use.

CHAPTER 7
Generative AI Architecture

Generative AI, a fascinating subset of artificial intelligence, has revolutionized how we create and interact with data. By mimicking patterns in data, generative models can produce new, unseen outputs.

This blog delves into the intricacies of Generative AI Architecture, exploring its core components, models, and applications. It discusses the significance of quality data, various generative models like GANs, VAEs, and transformers, and the essential layers involved in the architecture. This chapter also covers training techniques, evaluation metrics, and ethical considerations.

Overview Of Generative AI Architecture

Generative AI architecture refers to the overall structure and components involved in building and deploying generative AI models. While there can be variations based on specific use cases, a typical generative AI architecture consists of the key components.

Generative AI indicates to a category of AI models capable of creating media content. These models primarily rely on user-generated text prompts to generate content, but they can also create media in other forms, such as images. For example, the user must input Prompts like "From a theoretical perspective of human agency, write a 1,000-word literature review of the psychological resilience literature".

Generative AI, controlled by LLMs and text-to-image models, is rapidly improving. Models for audio, video, and music may mature soon. Large Language Models (LLMs) such as OpenAI's GPT and text-to-image models like Stable Diffusion have revolutionized the potential for generating data. By utilizing ChatGPT and Stable Diffusion, it is now possible to generate natural sounding text content and photorealistic images at an unprecedented scale. These models have proven to be capable of producing high-quality text and images.

Understanding generative AI architecture requires a peek behind the curtain, a deconstruction of the four pillars that hold it up

Main Pillars Of Generative AI Architecture:

Generative AI architecture refers to the overall structure and components of building and deploying generative AI models. While there can be variations based on specific use cases, a typical generative AI architecture consists of the following key components:

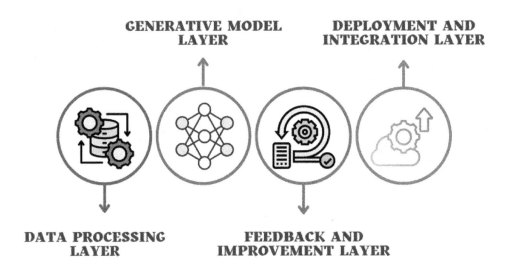

Components of Generative AI Architecture

1. Data Processing Layer

Data processing layer where raw material becomes canvas, this layer collects, prepares, and processes data for Generative AI models. Collection involves sourcing data from various outlets, preparation includes data cleaning and normalization, feature extraction identifies crucial data patterns, and the model is trained with processed data. Before the magic of creation begins, raw data like text, images, audio these all must be transformed into a language the model understands. This involves a delicate dance of cleaning, normalization, and transformation. Text gets scrubbed of errors and inconsistencies, images resized and adjusted, and audio waveforms sliced and encoded. Think of it as preparing the canvas for the artist, ensuring the highest quality materials for the masterpiece to come.

2. Generative Model Layer

This layer generates new content or data using machine learning models. It involves model selection based on the use case, training the models using relevant data, and fine-tuning them to optimize performance. The Generative model layer plays a pivotal role in enterprise Generative AI, creating new content using techniques like deep learning, reinforcement learning, or genetic algorithms tailored to the specific use case and data type. Within this layer lies the beating heart of the model – the algorithms that learn the hidden patterns and relationships within the data. From the adversarial dance of Generative Adversarial Networks (GANs) to the intricate compression and reconstruction of Variational Autoencoders (VAEs), these models are the architects of the unseen, shaping the raw material into novel forms.

3. Feedback and Improvement Layer

This layer focuses on continuously improving the generative model's accuracy and efficiency. It involves collecting user feedback, analyzing generated data, and using insights to drive improvements in the model.

The feedback and improvement layer, a vital component of enterprise generative AI, focuses on enhancing the model's accuracy and efficiency. Its effectiveness hinges on feedback quality and optimization techniques. User input gathered through surveys, behavior analysis, and interaction evaluation informs model optimization. Patterns and anomalies in generated data are identified using statistical analysis, data visualization, and machine learning tools. Optimization techniques encompass hyperparameter tuning, regularization (e.g., L1, L2), and transfer learning, fine-tuning pre-trained models for specific tasks. This iterative process ensures the model evolves to meet user expectations, enhancing performance and efficiency.

4. Deployment and Integration Layer

This layer integrates and deploys the generative model into the final product or system. It includes setting up a production infrastructure, integrating the model with application systems, and monitoring its performance. Once trained, the model graduates from the laboratory to the real world. This layer orchestrates its deployment into applications that span the spectrum of human experience. From powering image generation tools and personalized writing assistants to composing original music and designing innovative materials, the possibilities are as vast as the human imagination.

Understand Layers of Generative AI Architecture:

In a generative AI architecture platform, there are some layers that support the operations and performance of the application. The architecture of a generative AI system typically consists of multiple layers, each responsible for specific functions. While there may be variations based on specific use cases, a typical generative AI architecture includes the following key layers

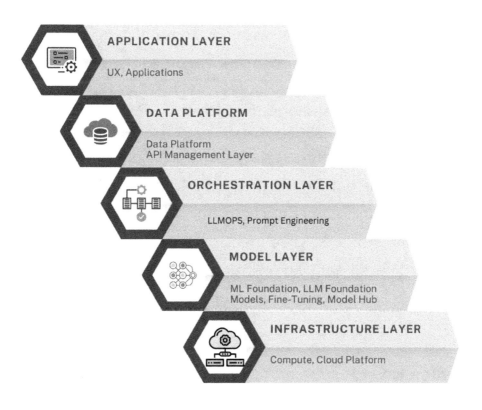

Layers of Generative AI Architecture

1. **Application layer**

The application layer in the generative AI tech stack enables humans and machines to collaborate seamlessly, making AI models accessible and easy to use. It can be classified into end-to-end apps using proprietary models and apps without proprietary models. End-to-end apps use proprietary generative AI models developed by companies with domain-specific expertise. Apps without proprietary models are built using open-source generative AI frameworks or libraries, enabling developers to build custom models for specific use cases. These tools democratize access to generative AI technology, fostering innovation and creativity.

2. **Data platform and API management layer**

High-quality data is crucial to achieve better outcomes in Gen AI. However, getting the data to the proper state takes up 70% of the development time, including data ingestion, cleaning, quality checks, vectorization, and storage. While many organizations have a data strategy for structured data, an unstructured data strategy is necessary to align with the Gen AI strategy and unlock value from unstructured data.

3. **Orchestration Layer**

LLMOps and Prompt Engineering is part of orchestration layer, LLMOps provides tooling, technologies, and practices for adapting and deploying models within end-user applications LLMOps include activities such as selecting a foundation model, adapting this model for your specific use case, evaluating the model, deploying it, and monitoring its performance. Adapting a foundation model is mainly done through prompt engineering or fine-tuning. Fine-tuning adds to the complexity by requiring data labeling, model training, and deployment to production. In the LLMOps space, several tools have emerged, including point solutions for experimentation, deployment, monitoring, observability, prompt engineering, governance, and end-to-end LLMOps tools.

4. Model layer and Hub

The model layer encompasses several models, including Machine Learning Foundation models, LLM Foundation models, fine-tuned models, and a model hub. Foundation models serve as the backbone of generative AI. These deep learning models are pre-trained to create specific types of content and can be adapted for various tasks. They require expertise in data preparation, model architecture selection, training, and tuning. Foundation models are trained on large datasets, both public and private. However, training these models is expensive; only a few tech giants and well-funded startups currently dominate the market. Model hubs are essential for businesses looking to build applications on top of foundation models. They provide a centralized location to access and store foundation and specialized models.

5. Infrastructure Layer

The infrastructure layer of generative AI models includes cloud platforms and hardware responsible for training and inference workloads. Traditional computer hardware cannot handle the massive amounts of data required to create content in generative AI systems. Large clusters of GPUs or TPUs with specialized accelerator chips are needed to process the data across billions of parameters in parallel. NVIDIA and Google dominate the chip design market, and TSMC produces almost all accelerator chips. Therefore, most businesses prefer to build, tune, and run large AI models in the cloud, where they can easily access computational power and manage their spending as needed. The major cloud providers have the most comprehensive platforms for running generative AI workloads and preferential access to hardware and chips.

Technology Of Generative AI

"Generative AI topology" refers to the structural design of a generative artificial intelligence model, essentially describing how different components like the "generator" and "discriminator" (in the case of GANs) are interconnected and work together to produce new data, often mimicking the patterns found in a training dataset; it outlines the overall architecture of the model, including the flow of information through different layers and the mathematical functions used to process data.

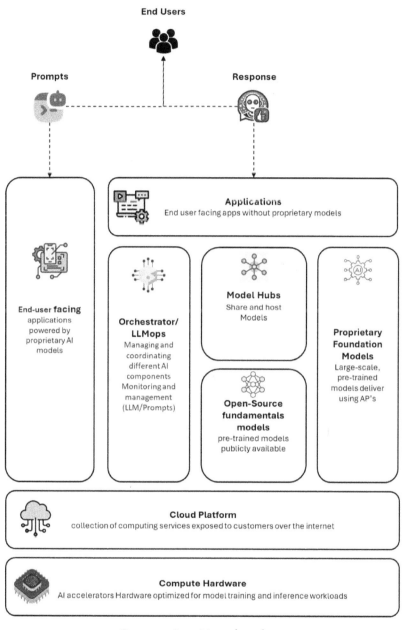

Generative AI technology

Generative AI technology , this illustration provides insight into the current state of the technological stack, with a focus on generative AI. this framework facilitates the analysis of generative AI technologies, categorizing them into distinct sections, each accompanied by a selection of well-established within the emerging landscape of generative AI, enterprises are engaged in developing proprietary models, leveraging third-party generative AI through APIs, or constructing applications by adapting finely-tuned open-source models to meet their specific needs.

End-User Facing Applications (Open-source)

leveraging generative AI without proprietary models often rely on open-source frameworks or libraries, enabling developers to build custom applications for specific use cases. These apps are built using tools like TensorFlow, PyTorch, or Keras, allowing for greater customization and flexibility compared to proprietary models.

Examples of such applications include:

- **RunwayML:** A platform for creating and sharing generative AI tools.
- **StyleGAN:** A generative adversarial network (GAN) used for image generation.
- **NeuralStyler:** An application for generating artistic styles.

Benefits of using open-source frameworks:

- **Accessibility:** Open-source frameworks democratize access to generative AI technology, making it available to a wider audience.
- **Customization:** Developers can tailor models to specific needs and use cases, enabling greater flexibility and control.
- **Innovation:** Open-source frameworks foster innovation and creativity by enabling developers to build unique and specialized applications.

How these applications work:

- Open-source frameworks provide the tools and resources for developers to build custom generative AI models.
- These models can be trained on specific datasets to generate outputs tailored to particular use cases.
- End-user facing applications leverage these models to create new content, solve problems, or enhance user experiences.

Examples of End-User Facing Apps without Proprietary Models:

- **Text generation tools:** These applications utilize open-source language models to generate creative text formats, such as poems, scripts, or marketing copy.
- **Image generation tools:** Tools like StyleGAN or neural filters allow users to generate images based on their input or prompts.
- **Music generation tools:** Some applications leverage open-source models to create new musical pieces or enhance existing ones.

- **Code generation tools:** These tools can help developers create code snippets or complete programs by leveraging open-source models.

these applications empower users to interact with generative AI technology without relying on proprietary models, offering greater flexibility, accessibility, and customization options.

End-user facing apps (powered by proprietary):

AI models are those that utilize AI models developed and owned by a specific company, offering a user-friendly interface and specific features accessible through the company's platform or API. These apps are designed to deliver a seamless and valuable experience to the end user by leveraging the power of AI in a way that is intuitive and easy to use.

Examples of such apps include:

- **Chatbots and virtual assistants:** These apps use proprietary AI models to understand user requests and respond with appropriate information or actions.

- **Image and video editing tools:** Apps like Adobe Photoshop or Canva use AI to enhance image quality, automate tasks, or generate new content.

- **Personalized recommendations:** E-commerce platforms and streaming services use AI to recommend products or content based on user preferences and past behavior.
- **Language translation tools:** Apps like Google Translate use AI to translate text between different languages.

Benefits of proprietary model apps:

- **User-friendly interface:** Proprietary models typically offer a polished and user-friendly interface that is easy to navigate and interact with.
- **Robust performance:** These models are often rigorously tested and optimized for performance, providing a smooth user experience.
- **Regular updates and support:** Companies maintain and update these models, ensuring that they are secure, reliable, and receive ongoing support.
- **Specialized functionality:** Proprietary models can be tailored to specific tasks or domains, providing advanced functionality that is not available with open-source models.
- **Data privacy:** Proprietary models can be designed to prioritize user data privacy and security.
- **Seamless integration:** Proprietary models can be easily integrated into existing applications or platforms, allowing for seamless user experience.

Considerations for end users:

- **Cost:** Access to proprietary models often requires payment, either through subscriptions or per-use fees.
- **Vendor lock-in:** Choosing a proprietary model can lead to vendor lock-in, making it difficult to migrate to other platforms or models in the future.
- **Data privacy concerns**: While proprietary models can prioritize data privacy, it's important to understand the company's data handling practices before using their services.

Orchestrator/LLMops

Generative AI orchestration or LLOps refers to the process of managing and coordinating different components within a generative AI system, essentially acting as a central control point to seamlessly integrate various functionalities like data retrieval, model selection, prompt engineering, and output processing, allowing for complex workflows and efficient execution of generative AI tasks across multiple steps and data sources.

Key points about generative AI orchestration:

- Workflow management: It automates the sequence of actions required to generate desired outputs, including chaining different generative models together depending on the task complexity.

- Data integration: Orchestration facilitates seamless access to diverse data sources, allowing generative models to leverage relevant information from across an organization.
- Model selection: It enables dynamic selection of the most suitable generative model based on specific use cases and input parameters.
- Prompt engineering: Orchestration can manage the crafting of effective prompts to guide the generative model towards desired results.
- Monitoring and feedback: It provides mechanisms to track the performance of generative models and adjust parameters based on feedback loops.

Why is orchestration important for generative AI?

- **Complex applications:** Generative AI often involves intricate workflows with multiple steps, requiring coordinated management.
- **Enterprise integration:** Orchestration allows seamless connection between generative models and existing enterprise systems and data sources.
- **Scalability:** By managing various components centrally, orchestration can efficiently scale generative AI applications to handle increased demand.

LLOps (Large Language Model Operations):

- **Subset of Generative AI Orchestration:** LLMOps specifically focuses on the operational aspects of deploying and managing large language models (LLMs) within a generative AI system.
- **Key aspects of LLMOps:** Model selection, fine-tuning, prompt engineering, deployment, monitoring, and governance of LLMs.

Proprietary Foundation Models

A closed source Foundational model in the context of generative AI refers to a large, powerful AI model developed by a company that keeps the underlying code, train ing data, and architecture completely private, meaning only the company developing it has access to the details and can utilize it, unlike open-source models which are publicly available for anyone to study and modify.

Key points about closed source fundamental models:

- **Proprietary information:** The company protects its intellectual property by not sharing the model's inner workings, allowing them to maintain a competitive edge.
- **Limited customization:** Users can only access the model through the company's API, often with restricted functionality and limited ability to fine-tune it for specific needs.

- **Potential for data privacy concerns:** Since the training data is not disclosed, users might have concerns about how their information is being used.

Why companies might choose closed source models:

- **Security concerns:** Sensitive data used to train the model may need to be protected from unauthorized access.
- **Commercial advantage:** Keeping the technology proprietary allows the company to monetize the model through exclusive services.

Examples of closed source generative AI models:

- **Google's LaMDA:** While some aspects of LaMDA are publicly discussed, the core model architecture remains mostly closed.
- **OpenAI's GPT-4:** While OpenAI has released some open-source models, their most advanced models like GPT-4 are primarily accessed through a paid API with limited control over the underlying technology.

Model Hubs

The most widely used platform for sharing generative AI models is Hugging Face; it provides a large community hub where users can discover, share, and access a vast library of pre-trained AI models, including language models, vision models, and more, making it a go-to platform for sharing and accessing various generative AI models.

Key points about Hugging Face:

- **Extensive Model Library:** Hosts a huge collection of open-source models contributed by the community, covering a wide range of tasks like natural language processing (NLP), computer vision, and speech recognition.
- **Easy to Use Interface:** Provides a user-friendly platform to upload, manage, and access models with detailed documentation and tutorials.
- **Community Driven:** Encourages collaboration and sharing within the AI community with features to discuss, rate, and review models.

Open-Source fundamentals models

Open source fundamentals models refers to large, pre-trained artificial intelligence models that are publicly available with open source code, allowing anyone to access, modify, and distribute them for various applications, with prominent examples including Llama, Falcon, Stable Diffusion, MPT 7b, and Dolly; essentially, these models serve as a foundational base for building custom AI systems while providing transparency in their development process.

Key points about open source fundamentals models:

- **Accessibility:** The code and model weights are freely available for anyone to use and adapt.
- **Flexibility:** Users can fine-tune the models for specific tasks by adjusting parameters and training on custom datasets.
- **Community-driven development:** Open source models benefit from contributions and improvements from a large developer community.

Some popular open source fundamentals models:

- **Llama (Meta):** A powerful language model optimized for conversational applications, with various fine-tuned versions like Japanese Llama
- **Falcon (Hugging Face):** A large language model known for its high performance and different parameter sizes, including a dedicated instruction model
- **Stable Diffusion (Stability AI):** A leading open-source text-to-image generation model capable of producing realistic images
- **MPT 7b (MosaicML):** A transformer-based model designed for fast training and inference with long input sequences
- **Dolly (Databricks):** Focuses on data analytics and machine learning tasks, well-suited for large datasets

Cloud Platform

A cloud platform is a collection of servers in a data center that provides cloud computing services to customers over the internet. Cloud platforms allow businesses to rent access to computing resources on demand, rather than buying and managing their own data centers and software.

Cloud platforms enable organizations to:

- Create cloud-native applications
- Test and build applications
- Store, back up, and recover data
- Analyze data
- Stream video and audio
- Deliver software on-demand on a global scale

Cloud computing allows users to access a wide range of technologies, including infrastructure services, machine learning, data lakes, and analytics. Users can quickly spin up resources as needed and deploy technology services in minutes.

The main types of cloud computing are public cloud, private cloud, and hybrid cloud. Some of the biggest cloud service providers include AWS, GCP, and Azure.

Compute Hardware

This tier encompasses the platforms and hardware (e.g., cloud platforms and hardware) responsible for executing training and inference workloads for generative AI models.

hardware that powers generative AI. Here's a breakdown of the key components:

Artificial Intelligence (AI) represents a revolutionary technology that mimics human intelligence, enabling machines to learn from experience, adapt to new information, and perform human-like tasks. The hardware is a cornerstone in unleashing AI's potential, providing the necessary computational resources to process and analyze vast amounts of data efficiently.

Processing Units:

- **GPUs (Graphics Processing Units):** These are the workhorses of generative AI, excelling at parallel processing, which is crucial for the complex matrix math involved in neural networks. NVIDIA is a dominant player in this space, with their GPUs and CUDA platform being widely used.

- **TPUs (Tensor Processing Units):** Developed by Google, TPUs are specifically designed for machine learning tasks, offering even greater efficiency than GPUs for certain workloads.
- **CPUs (Central Processing Units):** While not as central as GPUs or TPUs for the core AI computations, CPUs are still important for managing other aspects of the system, such as data loading and pre/post-processing.

Memory:

- **High-Bandwidth Memory (HBM):** Generative AI models require massive amounts of data to be readily accessible. HBM provides the necessary high bandwidth and low latency to feed data to the processing units efficiently.
- **VRAM (Video RAM):** This is the memory directly on the GPU. Larger VRAM capacity allows for working with larger models and datasets.

Interconnects:

- **High-speed Interconnects (e.g., NVLink):** These technologies enable fast communication between GPUs and other components, which is essential for scaling performance across multiple processors.

Storage:

- **Fast Storage (SSDs, NVMe drives):** For quick access to datasets and model checkpoints.

Hardware Considerations for Different Stages:

- **Training:** This is the most computationally intensive stage, requiring powerful data centers with many interconnected GPUs or TPUs, large amounts of HBM, and fast storage.
- **Inference:** This is the stage where the trained model is used to generate new content. The hardware requirements vary depending on the complexity of the model and the desired speed. It can range from cloud servers to personal computers with dedicated GPUs, and even mobile devices in some cases.

Key Factors to Consider:

- **Computational Power:** Measured in FLOPS (floating-point operations per second).
- **Memory Bandwidth:** The rate at which data can be transferred to and from memory.
- **Memory Capacity:** The amount of memory available.
- **Interconnect Speed:** The speed of communication between components.

generative AI relies on powerful and specialized hardware to handle the immense computational demands of training and running complex models. The field is constantly evolving, with new hardware innovations emerging to further accelerate progress in generative AI.

CHAPTER 8
Reference Architecture for GenAI Applications

The generative AI reference architecture provides a set of architectural building blocks that provides a blueprint for building end-to-end large language model based applications for the enterprise. as we go from the phases of proof of concept to production grade systems it is important to understand what the building blocks are and how to implement them. for each building block we provide that building block as a design pattern or architectural pattern in which we explore the various aspects of the problem, the context, the forces or trade-offs, the solution, the resulting consequence and possibly related patterns.

Reference Architecture for GenAI Applications

A reference architecture for GenAI applications provides a blueprint for building end-to-end systems that leverage the power of generative AI models. This architecture typically consists of several key components:

1. Data Ingestion and Preparation

- **Data Sources:** Identify and collect relevant data from various sources, such as databases, APIs, and cloud storage.
- **Data Cleaning and Transformation:** Cleanse the data by handling missing values, removing duplicates, and formatting inconsistencies. Transform the data into a suitable format for the chosen GenAI model.
- **Data Enrichment:** Enhance the data with additional information to improve model performance.

2. Model Selection and Training

- **Model Selection:** Choose the appropriate GenAI model based on the specific use case and data characteristics. Popular choices include Large Language Models (LLMs), Generative Adversarial Networks (GANs), and Variational Autoencoders (VAEs).
- **Model Training:** Train the selected model on the prepared data using appropriate training techniques. This may involve fine-tuning pre-trained models or training from scratch.

- **Hyperparameter Tuning:** Optimize model parameters to improve performance and efficiency.

3. Model Serving and Inference

- **Model Deployment:** Deploy the trained model to a production environment for real-time inference. This may involve using cloud-based services or on-premises infrastructure.
- **API Gateway:** Create an API gateway to manage incoming requests, authenticate users, and route requests to the appropriate model.
- **Inference Engine:** Process user inputs, generate outputs, and return results to the client.

4. User Interface and Integration

- **User Interface:** Design an intuitive and user-friendly interface for interacting with the GenAI application. This may include web applications, chatbots, or other interactive interfaces.
- **Integration:** Integrate the GenAI application with other systems and tools to enhance its functionality. This may involve connecting to databases, business applications, or other AI services.

5. Monitoring and Maintenance

- **Performance Monitoring:** Monitor the performance of the GenAI application, including response times, accuracy, and resource utilization.

- **Model Retraining:** Regularly retrain the model with new data to maintain accuracy and relevance.
- **Security and Compliance:** Implement security measures to protect the model and user data, and ensure compliance with relevant regulations.

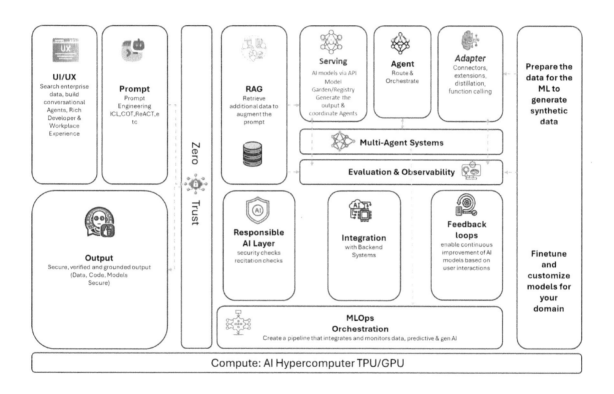

reference architecture diagram for GenAI applications

Key Considerations:

- **Scalability:** Design the architecture to handle increasing demand and scale efficiently as needed.

- **Ethical Implications:** Consider the ethical implications of the GenAI application, such as bias, fairness, and privacy.
- **Security:** Implement robust security measures to protect the model and user data.
- **Cost-Effectiveness:** Optimize the architecture to minimize costs associated with data storage, model training, and inference.

By following these guidelines and adapting the architecture to specific requirements, organizations can build effective and scalable GenAI applications that deliver real business value.

GenAI Reference Architecture Artifacts

UI/UX

Users interact with AI through various channels, including search engines, chatbots, and enterprise software. As AI becomes integrated into daily tools, a seamless experience is crucial. For instance, a user might interact with an AI-powered search engine and then transition to a conversational agent for more complex queries, expecting a cohesive and consistent experience.

Designing UI/UX for AI involves balancing simplicity and functionality. The interface should be easy to use while providing access to powerful AI features. Trade-offs include deciding between a simple interface with limited functions versus a complex one that may overwhelm users. A well-designed interface strikes a balance, enabling users to efficiently utilize AI capabilities.

Prompt engineering

Prompt engineering is the art of crafting effective instructions for generative AI models to produce the desired output. AI models, especially large language models, rely on prompts to understand and generate text. The quality of prompts directly impacts the accuracy and relevance of the model's output. Well-engineered prompts are essential for tasks like text generation, question-answering, and language translation.

- Designing and refining inputs (prompts) to guide AI models like large language models (LLMs) to generate specific and high-quality outputs.
- It's about communicating your intent clearly and precisely to the AI.

Why it's important:

- **Improved Output Quality:** Well-crafted prompts lead to more accurate, relevant, and creative responses from the AI.
- **Efficiency:** Clear instructions save time and effort by minimizing the need for multiple attempts or revisions.
- **Control and Direction:** Prompt engineering allows you to guide the AI's output towards specific styles, formats, and levels of detail.

Key Techniques:

- **Clear and Concise Instructions:** Be specific about the desired output (e.g., "Write a short story about a robot who dreams of becoming a chef").
- **Provide Context:** Include relevant background information or examples to guide the AI's understanding.

- **Use Specific Keywords and Phrases:** Guide the AI's tone, style, and level of formality (e.g., "Write a humorous poem," "Explain in simple terms").
- **Break Down Complex Tasks:** For complex requests, break them down into smaller, more manageable sub-tasks.
- **Iterative Refinement:** Experiment with different prompts and refine them based on the AI's output.

Example:

Poor Prompt: "Tell me about India."

These examples demonstrate how vague, ambiguous, or poorly defined prompts can lead to unpredictable or irrelevant outputs from generative AI models.

Improved Prompt: "Write a concise travel guide for first-time visitors to India, highlighting key attractions, cultural experiences, and local cuisine."

This prompt is improved because, specificity, clarity, clear input This improved prompt will likely result in a more accurate and relevant output from the AI model.

Detailed prompts provide clear guidance to AI models, improving accuracy. However, overly specific prompts may limit flexibility and creativity. Finding the right balance ensures the model can adapt to various situations while producing desired outputs.

By using effective prompt engineering techniques, you can unlock the full potential of generative AI models and achieve exceptional results in various applications, from content creation and research to customer service and software development.

RAG (Retrieve, Augment, Generate)

Retrieval-Augmented Generation (RAG) is a powerful technique that enhances the capabilities of large language models (LLMs) by combining them with information retrieval systems.

How RAG Works:

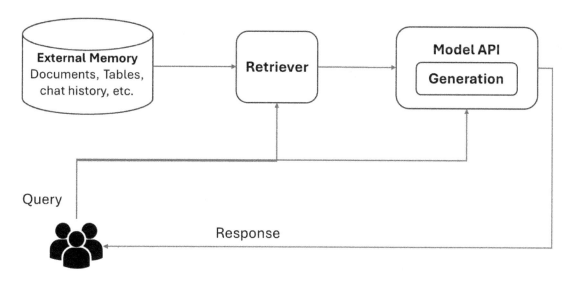

The most well-known pattern for context construction is RAG, Retrieval-Augmented Generation. RAG consists of two components: a generator (e.g. a language model) and a retriever, which retrieves relevant information from external sources.

AI models, especially language models, rely on prompts for context. Incomplete prompts can result in inaccurate or incomplete responses. RAG aims to provide a richer context by retrieving and incorporating additional data.

- **Retrieval:** When a user query is received, the RAG system first retrieves relevant information from an external knowledge base. This knowledge base could be a collection of documents, a database, or any other source of information.
- **Augmentation:** The retrieved information is then used to augment the input to the LLM. This could involve:
    - **Concatenation:** Simply appending the retrieved information to the user query.
    - **Contextualization:** Providing the retrieved information as context to the LLM, allowing it to generate responses that are more relevant and informative.
- **Generation:** Finally, the LLM generates a response based on the augmented input. This response is typically more accurate, informative, and relevant than what the LLM could generate on its own.

Benefits of RAG:

- **Improved Accuracy and Factuality**: By accessing external knowledge, RAG systems can generate more accurate and factually correct responses.
- **Enhanced Relevance:** RAG allows LLMs to generate responses that are more relevant to the specific context of the user query.

- **Improved Informativeness:** RAG enables LLMs to provide more comprehensive and informative responses by incorporating relevant information from external sources.
- **Domain-Specific Knowledge:** RAG can be used to incorporate domain-specific knowledge into LLMs, making them more effective for tasks such as customer service, research, and legal analysis.

Applications of RAG:

- **Chatbots and Conversational AI:** RAG can be used to create more informative and accurate chatbots that can access and utilize a wide range of information sources.
- **Question Answering Systems:** RAG can be used to build powerful question-answering systems that can provide accurate and comprehensive answers to user queries.
- **Content Generation:** RAG can be used to generate high-quality content, such as news articles, product descriptions, and marketing materials, that are informed by relevant data.
- **Research and Development:** RAG can be used to assist researchers in finding relevant information and generating new insights.

Key Considerations:

- **Data Quality:** The quality of the retrieved information is crucial for the effectiveness of RAG systems.
- **Retrieval Efficiency:** Efficient retrieval methods are essential for real-time applications.

- **Bias and Fairness:** It's important to address potential biases in the retrieved information and ensure that RAG systems generate fair and unbiased responses.

RAG empowers LLMs by connecting them to the vast amount of information available on the web and in other knowledge bases. This allows LLMs to go beyond their pre-trained knowledge and generate more accurate, informative, and relevant responses.

Serving AI Models

Model serving is one of the critical steps of model deployment and should not be neglected. Model training is relatively conventional, with a well-known set of tools and methodologies for utilizing them, such as scikit-learn, xgboost, and others. The deployment of models is the polar opposite. Your deployment strategy and infrastructure are intricately linked to user expectations, business regulations, and existing technology at your company.

Serving AI models to the process of deploying and making trained machine learning models accessible for use in production environments. This involves making the model available to receive inputs and generate predictions or inferences. Serving, or deploying, the output of AI models to end-users or systems is a critical step in the AI development process.

Once an AI model is trained, its output needs to be delivered in a usable format to provide value to users or other systems.

Implement a serving layer that hosts the AI model and exposes its functionality via an API, allowing applications to access and integrate AI capabilities.

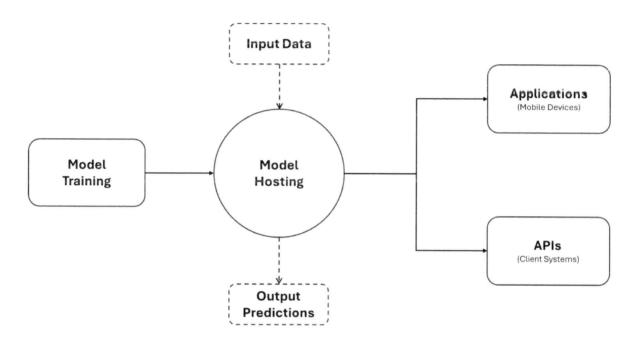

Serving of models from training environment to the end user

Machine learning has the potential to transform businesses and take them to great heights. Still, it is possible only when models are put into production and consumers can easily interact with them. Deploying machine learning models into production comprises several sub-tasks, each of which is crucial in its own right.

Model serving is one of these sub-tasks.

It is a technique for integrating a machine learning model into a software system. In other words, you can say that it is the process of exposing a trained model to an endpoint (say, end-users).

Model serving simply means hosting machine-learning models (on the cloud or on-premises) and making their functions available via API so that applications can integrate AI into their systems. With this action, you can use the machine learning model with just a few clicks. Model serving is critical as businesses cannot deliver AI solutions to an extensive user base without making them accessible.

Generally, models take a long time to go from a prototype to a production state. But with model serving, you may easily do that in a few minutes.

Model Serving accepts data science-standard formats for your models. ONNX (Open neural network exchange), PMML (Predictive model markup language), and TensorFlow are examples of these formats.

Some popular tools to help you in your model serving journey are Cortex, Seldon Core, KFServing, Streamlit, MLFlow, and BentoML.

Model Serving Strategies

Following are some of the common model serving strategies used by ML professionals:

1. **Offline Serving:** The end-user is not immediately exposed to your model in this method. It works by performing a batch inference job on your test dataset, caching the findings in a high-performance database, and then serving those results to end-users. The most significant downside of offline serving is that it is a "cold" deployment.
   It usually only works in 'push' workflows, where the end-user only accepts requests from the model server but does not create any requests. Offline serving can be used in 'pull' workflows where the end-user can send requests to the model server. It's challenging to implement because end-users often have unrealistic expectations regarding response times.

2. **Online model as service:** When a model learns from human input automatically, it is said to be online. A neural network with a batch size of one is a canonical example of online machine learning. A complete backpropagation pass is started based on the input each time a user requests to your model endpoint, changing the model weights simultaneously with serving the request.

3. **Model as Service:** The most typical model serving strategy in production environments is to deploy a model as a (micro)service. Clients are given access to a model interface via an API endpoint in this paradigm (REST or otherwise). Clients send POST or GET queries to the endpoint to get what they need. This is a scalable, responsive

model service deployment technique with a flexible deployment strategy.

4. **Edge deployment:** It refers to serving the model directly on the client device rather than on the server because it shifts the computation from the server to the edge (the client device). It's tricky since the client's hardware (a web browser, a user computer, or a mobile device) is severely limited.

Key aspects of Model Serving:

Deployment:

- Choosing the right infrastructure (cloud, on-premises, edge devices) to host the model.
- Packaging the model for deployment in a suitable format.
- Ensuring seamless integration with existing systems and applications.

Inference:

- Handling incoming requests for predictions.
- Efficiently processing input data and generating outputs.
- Optimizing for latency and throughput to meet performance requirements.

Monitoring and Maintenance:

- Continuously monitoring model performance, including latency, throughput, and accuracy.
- Detecting and addressing issues such as model drift, data degradation, and hardware failures.
- Implementing strategies for model updates and retraining.

Why is Model Serving Important?

- **Real-time Predictions:** Enables real-time applications that require immediate responses, such as fraud detection, recommendation systems, and autonomous vehicles.
- **Scalability and Flexibility:** Handle varying levels of traffic and adapt to changing demands.
- **Improved User Experience:** Deliver faster and more accurate predictions, leading to improved user satisfaction.
- **Increased Efficiency:** Automate tasks, reduce manual effort, and improve operational efficiency.
- **Competitive Advantage:** Gain a competitive edge by leveraging AI-powered applications and services.

Model serving is the bridge between the development of a machine learning model and its real-world application. It allows businesses to leverage the power of AI to make data-driven decisions, improve customer experiences, and gain a competitive advantage.

Adapt Modular AI

Modular AI components refer to designing artificial intelligence systems by breaking them down into smaller, independent units (modules) that can be easily combined, reused across different applications, and adapted to new situations without needing to rebuild the entire system, ultimately enhancing flexibility and scalability in AI development.

As AI continues to evolve and become more prevalent, AI solutions must be versatile and flexible to handle various functions and integrate seamlessly with existing systems.

Key points about modular AI components:

- **Reusability:** Individual modules can be used in various projects or parts of a larger system, saving development time and ensuring consistency across applications.
- **Adaptability:** By swapping or updating specific modules, the overall AI system can be adjusted to meet new requirements or changing environments without major overhauls.
- **Scalability:** Individual modules can be scaled independently based on workload, allowing for efficient resource allocation depending on the specific needs of the application.
- **Maintainability:** Easier to identify and fix issues within a modular system as changes are localized to specific components.

Examples of Modular AI Components:

- **Data preprocessing modules:** Handling data cleaning, transformation, and feature engineering.
- **Model training modules:** Implementing different training algorithms and hyperparameter tuning strategies.
- **Inference modules:** Handling input/output, model loading, and prediction generation.
- **Monitoring and logging modules:** Tracking model performance and generating reports.

By embracing modularity, organizations can unlock the full potential of AI and build more sophisticated and impactful AI applications.

Modular AI components significantly enhance adaptability and reusability in several ways:

1. **Increased Flexibility:**

- **Component Swapping:** Need to change the underlying model? No problem! With modularity, you can easily swap out one model for another without affecting the overall system architecture. This is crucial as AI models are constantly evolving.
- **Customizable Pipelines:** Build flexible pipelines by combining different modules for data preprocessing, feature engineering, model training, and inference. This allows for easy experimentation and optimization.

2. Improved Maintainability:

- **Isolation of Changes:** When changes are needed, they can be isolated to specific modules, minimizing the risk of unintended consequences in other parts of the system.
- **Easier Debugging:** If a problem arises, it's easier to pinpoint the source of the issue within a specific module.

3. Enhanced Reusability:

- **Pre-built Components:** Many common AI tasks (e.g., image preprocessing, text tokenization) can be encapsulated in reusable modules. This saves development time and effort across projects.
- **Shared Libraries:** Create libraries of reusable AI components that can be shared within a team or even across an organization.

4. Faster Development:

- **Leveraging Existing Work:** By reusing existing modules, developers can accelerate the development process and focus on building unique and innovative applications.
- **Parallel Development:** Different teams can work on different modules independently, speeding up the overall development cycle.

modularity in AI promotes a more efficient, flexible, and maintainable development process. It allows for faster innovation, easier experimentation, and the creation of more robust and adaptable AI systems

Example of modular AI in practice:

- **Natural Language Processing (NLP):** A modular AI system might have separate modules for text cleaning, sentiment analysis, and topic extraction, allowing developers to easily integrate the relevant NLP functions into different projects based on their needs.
- **Computer Vision:** Different modules could handle image recognition, object detection, and facial analysis, enabling customization of a vision system based on the specific use case.

Modular AI components enhance adaptability and reusability and System Integration Integrating AI solutions with existing systems is crucial for seamless adoption.

AI solutions need to be adaptable to different use cases and environments to meet diverse user needs and expectations. As AI continues to evolve and become more prevalent, AI solutions must be versatile and flexible to handle various functions and integrate seamlessly with existing systems.

The solution is extend and distill AI solutions by developing modular components and connectors that allow integration with different systems. Continuously evaluate the performance of AI solutions in various environments and use cases.

- Adopt adaptive AI solutions that can learn from new data and improve themselves over time, eliminating the need for intensive programming and manual coding when making updates.

- Utilize continuous learning paradigms to enable AI systems to become more efficient, scalable, and sustainable.
- Leverage data science staff to help parse insights from data sets and provide follow-on predictions, recommendations, and projected outcomes.

AI solutions that are robust and adaptable, able to meet a wide range of enterprise environments and user needs, enhancing customer satisfaction and flexibility.

Feedback loops and continuous monitoring

Feedback loops and continuous monitoring allow AI models to continuously improve by creating a cycle where user interactions are captured as feedback, analyzed to identify areas for improvement, and then used to retrain the model, resulting in better performance over time as the AI learns from its mistakes and adapts to changing user behavior; essentially, the system is constantly "listening" to user input and adjusting its responses accordingly, leading to a more refined and user-friendly experience

Ensuring the accuracy, relevance, and ethical soundness of AI outputs is crucial for their effective utilization.

As AI systems are increasingly deployed in critical areas, the relevance and accuracy of their outputs directly impact their usefulness and societal impact.

AI governance layer that includes unbiased safety checks, recitation checks, and oversight mechanisms. There is a trade-off between achieving highly accurate AI outputs and ensuring the breadth of their knowledge and capabilities.

Solution is to Implement evaluation and validation mechanisms to assess the quality, performance, and bias of AI outputs, grounding them in additional data and validations.

- Utilize automated monitoring systems to detect bias, drift, performance issues, and anomalies in AI models, ensuring they function correctly and ethically.
- Establish performance alerts to enable timely interventions when a model deviates from its predefined performance parameters.
- Implement feedback loops to address user frustrations and keep them engaged, guiding them toward accuracy and preventing them from getting stuck.

The quality of the data used for training, fine-tuning and the information retrievable using RAG for LLMs are key-determinants of the quality of the model output.

Generative AI feedback loops and continuous monitoring allow AI models to constantly improve by collecting user interaction data, analyzing it to identify areas for improvement, and then using that feedback to refine the model's parameters, effectively creating a cycle where the AI learns and adapts to user behavior over time, leading to more accurate and relevant outputs

Key aspects of this process:

- **Collecting User Feedback:** When users interact with a generative AI model, their actions and responses are captured as data, which can include explicit feedback like ratings or comments, or implicit feedback like which options users choose or how they navigate the interface.
- **Analyzing Feedback:** This data is then analyzed to identify patterns and trends, pinpointing areas where the model is performing well or where it needs improvement.
- **Model Adjustment:** Based on the feedback analysis, the AI model's parameters are adjusted, allowing it to better understand user intent and generate more relevant outputs in the future.
- **Continuous Monitoring:** The process doesn't stop there; the model's performance is continuously monitored to track how well it's adapting to new user interactions and to identify any emerging issues or biases.

Benefits of Generative AI Feedback Loops:

- **Improved Accuracy:** By learning from user interactions, the AI model can become more accurate in its responses, generating outputs that better align with user expectations.
- **Personalization:** Feedback loops allow the AI to tailor its responses to individual users based on their past interactions, creating a more personalized experience.
- **Adaptability to Change:** As user behavior evolves, the feedback loop enables the AI to adapt and learn new patterns, staying relevant over time.

Examples of Feedback Loops in Generative AI:

- **Chatbots:** When a user interacts with a chatbot, their questions and responses are logged, allowing the chatbot to improve its understanding of user queries and provide more accurate answers in the future.
- **Recommendation Systems:** Online platforms like Netflix or Amazon use user feedback (likes, dislikes, watched content) to refine their recommendation algorithms, suggesting items more likely to be of interest to each user.

Important Considerations:

- **Data Quality:** The quality of feedback data is crucial for effective model improvement.
- **Bias Mitigation:** Mechanisms should be in place to prevent the AI from learning and reinforcing biases present in user feedback.
- **Transparency and User Control:** Users should be informed about how their data is being used and have some control over how the AI learns from their interactions.

Prepare & Tune Data & Models

Preparing and tuning data and models" in the context of generative AI means meticulously cleaning, structuring, and adjusting a dataset to specifically fit the needs of a generative model, allowing it to produce highly relevant and accurate outputs for a particular task or domain, essentially tailoring the model to perform optimally for your specific use case by fine-tuning its parameters based on your curated data.

Preparing and tuning data and models is a crucial aspect of developing effective AI solutions. Efficient data pipelines play a vital role in this process, as they enable the necessary data cleaning, integration, and feature engineering tasks.

Key points about preparing and tuning data for generative AI:

- **Data Collection:** Gathering a large, diverse, and high-quality dataset that represents the desired output style and context for your generative model.
- **Data Cleaning:** Removing inconsistencies, duplicates, errors, and irrelevant information from the dataset to ensure the model learns from reliable data.
- **Data Preprocessing:** Transforming data into a format suitable for the model, including normalization, tokenization, and feature engineering.

- **Data Splitting:** Dividing the dataset into training, validation, and testing sets to evaluate model performance during training and fine-tuning.
- **Fine-Tuning:** Further training a pre-trained generative model on your specific dataset to adapt its parameters and focus its output towards your desired application

- **Data Preparation**
    - **Data Collection:**

        a. **High-Quality Data:** Crucial for generative AI, as the model learns from the data it's trained on.

        b. **Diverse and Representative:** The data should be diverse, representing various styles, topics, and perspectives to avoid biases and enhance creativity.

        c. **Clean and Organized:** Data should be free from errors, inconsistencies, and irrelevant information.

    - **Data Cleaning:**

        a. **Handle Missing Values:** Impute missing values using appropriate techniques (e.g., mean, median, imputation algorithms).

        b. **Remove Noise and Outliers:** Identify and remove outliers or noisy data that can negatively impact model training.

        c. **Correct Inaccuracies:** Address inconsistencies, errors, and biases in the data.

- **Data Preprocessing:**
  a. **Text Data:**
     - **Tokenization:** Break down text into smaller units (words, subwords).
     - **Cleaning:** Remove punctuation, stop words, and handle special characters.
     - **Lowercasing:** Convert text to lowercase for consistency.
  b. **Image Data:**
     - **Resize:** Resize images to a consistent size.
     - **Data Augmentation:** Increase data diversity by applying transformations like rotations, flips, and crops.
- **Data Splitting: Divide the data into:**
  a. **Training Set:** Used to train the model.
  b. **Validation Set:** Used to tune hyperparameters and evaluate model performance during training.
  c. **Test Set:** Used to evaluate the final model's performance on unseen data.
- **Model Tuning**
  - **Hyperparameter Tuning:**
    a. **Identify Key Hyperparameters:** Determine the model parameters that significantly impact performance (e.g., learning rate, number of layers, batch size).

b. **Search Strategies:** Explore different hyperparameter combinations using techniques like:
  - **Grid Search:** Evaluate model performance on a grid of hyperparameter values.
  - **Random Search:** Randomly sample hyperparameter values.
  - **Bayesian Optimization:** Use Bayesian methods to efficiently explore the hyperparameter space.

- **Fine-tuning Pre-trained Models:**
  a. **Start with a Strong Foundation:** Begin with a pre-trained model (like GPT-3, BERT) and fine-tune it on a smaller, more specific dataset relevant to the desired task.
  b. **Faster Training:** Fine-tuning often requires less data and computational resources compared to training a model from scratch.

- **Model Evaluation:**
  a. **Choose Appropriate Metrics:** Select metrics relevant to the specific task (e.g., perplexity, BLEU score for text generation, FID for image generation).
  b. **Evaluate Model Performance:** Monitor metrics on the validation set during training and use them to guide hyperparameter tuning.

- **Regularization:** Techniques to prevent overfitting:
  a. **Dropout:** Randomly drop out neurons during training to prevent over-reliance on specific features.

b. **Weight Decay:** Penalize large weights in the model to encourage simpler models.

Key Considerations for Generative AI:

- **Data Quality is Paramount:** The quality and diversity of the training data directly impact the quality and creativity of the generated output.
- **Computational Resources:** Training large generative AI models can be computationally expensive.
- **Ethical Considerations:** Ensure the data used for training is unbiased and does not perpetuate harmful stereotypes.

By carefully preparing and tuning data and models, you can significantly improve the performance, creativity, and safety of your generative AI systems.

Importance of Synthetic Data Generation in Fine-Tuning LLMs

1. **Data Augmentation:** Real-world datasets often suffer from class imbalances or limited representation of certain scenarios. Synthetic data generation can be used to augment the training datasets by creating new examples that balance the class distributions and cover underrepresented cases. This leads to more robust and generalized LLMs that perform well across diverse tasks and scenarios.
2. **Data Privacy and Security:** In many applications, real-world data may contain sensitive or personally identifiable information (PII). Synthetic data generation allows researchers to create datasets that retain the

essential statistical properties of the real data while ensuring privacy and security. By training LLMs on synthetic data, the risk of exposing sensitive information is significantly reduced.

3. **Exploration of Rare or Dangerous Scenarios:** Real-world data may lack examples of rare or dangerous events, making it challenging to train LLMs to handle such situations effectively. Synthetic data generation enables the creation of scenarios that are difficult or impossible to collect in real life, such as extreme weather events, accidents, or cyberattacks. By exposing LLMs to these synthetic scenarios during training, their ability to understand and respond to such events is enhanced.

4. **Cost and Time Efficiency:** Collecting and annotating large amounts of real-world data can be a time-consuming and expensive process. Synthetic data generation offers a cost-effective and efficient alternative by automating the data creation process. This allows researchers and developers to quickly iterate and experiment with different training scenarios, leading to faster model development and improvement.

5. **Customization and Control:** Synthetic data generation provides a high degree of customization and control over the data characteristics. Researchers can fine-tune the parameters of the data generation models to create datasets that meet specific requirements, such as controlling the diversity, complexity, or difficulty of the generated examples. This enables targeted fine-tuning of LLMs for specific applications or domains.

Ethical Considerations

While synthetic data generation offers significant advantages, it is crucial to consider the ethical implications associated with its use. Synthetic data should be used responsibly and transparently, ensuring that it does not perpetuate biases or misrepresentations present in the real data. Additionally, it is essential to validate the quality and representativeness of the synthetic data to ensure that it aligns with the characteristics of the real-world data it aims to simulate.

Raw data often requires cleaning and preparation to ensure it is complete, consistent, timely, and relevant. Models need to be fine-tuned for specific industry domains and use cases.

Tailored AI solutions that perform optimally for specific industry domains and use cases, addressing the unique needs and requirements of organizations.

Multi-Agent Systems

Multi-agent systems (MAS) have emerged as a powerful paradigm for building complex, modular, and scalable AI applications. As an experienced practitioner in this field, I've witnessed firsthand the evolution and impact of multi-agent architectures across various domains. This comprehensive guide aims to share deep insights into the world of multi-agent systems, drawing from both theoretical foundations and real-world implementations.

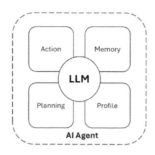

Single-Agent vs. Multi-Agent Systems

Before deep diving into multi-agent architectures, it's crucial to understand the limitations of single-agent systems that led to the development of MAS:

- **Single-Agent Systems:**

  In a single-agent system, a centralized agent makes all decisions, while other agents act as remote slaves.

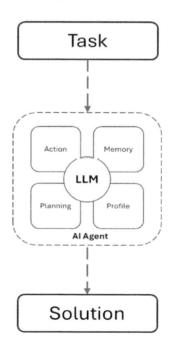

This single agent, normally decides, based on the context. This might miss out the other perspectives/possibilities. On the other hand, multi-agent systems involve multiple interacting intelligent agents, each capable of making decisions and influencing the environment.

- Utilize a single LLM to interact with tools and users for task completion.
- Effective for small-scale applications but face challenges as complexity grows:
    - **Tool overload:** Too many tools can overwhelm the agent, leading to poor decision-making.
    - **Context window limitations:** As interactions increase, the context becomes too large for the LLM to handle effectively.
    - **Lack of specialization:** A single agent may not perform optimally across diverse tasks.

- **Multi-Agent Systems:**

The idea behind multi-agent architecture is to create agents, with different contexts to bring in different perspectives, by the role they play. Though they might be using the same LLM, but due to the role, goal and the context that is defined for that agent, they behave differently. Just like a member in the team.

- Address the limitations of single-agent systems by distributing tasks across multiple specialized agents.
- Each agent can focus on a specific domain, improving modularity, scalability, and control.

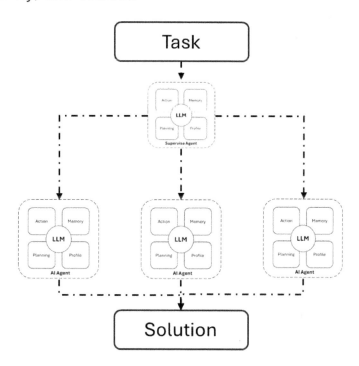

At its core, a multi-agent system is a collection of independent agents that interact with each other to perform tasks. In the context of AI, an agent is typically defined as a system that uses a large language model (LLM) to decide the control flow of an application.

Multi-agent systems differ from single-agent systems primarily in the distribution of decision-making and interaction within a system. In a single-agent system, a centralized agent makes all decisions, while other agents act as remote slaves. This single agent, normally decides, based on the context. This might miss out the other perspectives/possibilities. On the other hand, multi-agent systems involve multiple interacting intelligent agents, each capable of making decisions and influencing the environment.

The idea behind multi-agent architecture is to create agents, with different contexts to bring in different perspective, by the role they play. Though they might be using the same LLM, but due to the role, goal and the context that is defined for that agent, they behave different. Just like a member in the team.

Imagine you have an agent, that generates application code, another agent that reviews the code and they both get into a chat with each other to improve the code. Over a defined set of iterations, these two agents will come up with the best results. This approach has a huge potential, to not only generate a more satisfactory output, but also reduce the effects of Hallucinations, Bias etc. Defining the right context, prompt, with right model, in a multi-agent architecture is very critical. Strong prompt engineering skills help in designing an impactful multi-agent application.

Benefits of Multi-Agent Designs:

- **Separation of concerns**: Each agent can have its own instructions and few-shot examples, powered by separate fine-tuned language models, and supported by various tools. Dividing tasks among agents leads to better results. Each agent can focus on a specific task rather than selecting from a multitude of tools.

- **Modularity**: Multi-agent designs allow breaking down complex problems into manageable units of work, targeted by specialized agents and language models. Multi-agent designs allow you to evaluate and improve each agent independently without disrupting the entire application. Grouping tools and responsibilities can lead to better outcomes. Agents are more likely to succeed when focused on specific tasks.
- **Diversity**: Bring in strong diversity in the agent-teams to bring in different perspectives and refine the output and avoid Hallucinations & Bias. (Like a typical human team).
- **Reusability**: Once the agents are built, there is an opportunity to reuse these agents for different use cases, and think of an ecosystem of agents, that can come together to solve the problem, with a proper choreography/orchestration framework (such as AutoGen, Crew.ai etc)

Multi-agent systems have emerged as a powerful paradigm for designing and implementing complex AI systems. In MAS, multiple intelligent agents interact and collaborate to solve problems that are beyond the capabilities of individual agents.

Large Language Models (LLMs) have demonstrated remarkable capabilities in natural language understanding and generation. However, as the complexity of tasks and the need for specialized knowledge increase, leveraging multi-agent systems within LLMs can lead to more efficient and effective solutions.

Develop multi-agent systems that leverage the power of multiple intelligent agents working together to solve complex problems. Implement techniques for effective coordination, communication, and decision-making among agents.

In this blog we will only cover the basics and will provide details for a pattern language on Multi-agent systems in a subsequent blog. Stay tuned.

Develop a multi-agent architecture for LLMs that allows multiple specialized language models to collaborate and share knowledge. Implement techniques for effective communication, coordination, and decision-making among the agents to enable seamless integration and optimal performance.

Responsible/Governance AI

Governing AI systems refers to the processes, standards, and guardrails that ensure AI systems are developed, deployed, and used in a responsible, ethical, and safe manner. It involves establishing frameworks, policies, and practices to address the unique challenges and risks posed by AI technologies.

As AI systems become more powerful and pervasive, managing them responsibly and ethically becomes essential to prevent potential harm.AI systems can have significant societal impact, affecting individuals' rights, privacy, and dignity. Governance ensures AI systems operate within ethical and legal boundaries.

Implement a responsible AI governance layer that includes unbiased safety checks, recitation checks, and oversight mechanisms.

Key Aspects of Governing AI Systems:

1. **Ethical Considerations:** AI systems should align with human values, respect human rights, and avoid perpetuating biases or discrimination. Ethical guidelines and principles are crucial for guiding AI development and deployment.
2. **Legal Compliance:** AI systems must comply with existing laws and regulations, including those related to data privacy, intellectual property, and consumer protection. New legislation may be needed to address specific challenges posed by AI.
3. **Risk Management:** AI systems can pose various risks, including safety risks, privacy risks, and economic risks. Effective risk management frameworks are needed to identify, assess, and mitigate these risks.
4. **Transparency and Explainability:** AI systems should be transparent in their decision-making processes, and their outputs should be explainable to humans. This is crucial for building trust and accountability.
5. **Accountability and Oversight:** Clear lines of accountability should be established for AI systems, and mechanisms for human oversight and intervention should be in place.

6. **Technical Standards and Best Practices:** Technical standards and best practices are needed to ensure the quality, reliability, and security of AI systems.

7. **Stakeholder Engagement:** Governing AI systems requires engagement with a wide range of stakeholders, including researchers, developers, policymakers, businesses, and the public.

Why is Governing AI Systems Important?

- **Mitigating Risks:** AI systems can pose significant risks if not developed and used responsibly. Governance helps to mitigate these risks and prevent harm.
- **Building Trust:** Trust is essential for the widespread adoption of AI technologies. Effective governance helps to build trust by ensuring that AI systems are safe, reliable, and ethical.
- **Promoting Innovation:** Clear and consistent governance frameworks can provide a stable environment for AI innovation to flourish.
- **Ensuring Fairness and Equity:** Governance can help to ensure that AI systems are used in a fair and equitable manner, avoiding discrimination and bias.
- **Protecting Human Rights:** AI systems should be used in a way that respects human rights and fundamental freedoms

Governing AI systems is a complex and evolving field. It requires ongoing dialogue and collaboration among various stakeholders to ensure that AI technologies are used for the benefit of society.

MLOps

MLOps is a collection of practices for data professionals and operations professionals to collaborate and communicate. Using these practices improves the quality of Machine Learning and Deep Learning algorithms, simplifies management, and automates their deployment in large-scale production environments. Models are easier to align with business needs as well as compliance standards. MLOps is gradually evolving into a stand-alone methodology to ML life - cycle management. It covers the entire lifecycle, including data collection, model creation (SDLC, CI/CD), orchestration, implementation, health, diagnostic tests, governance, and performance measurement systems.

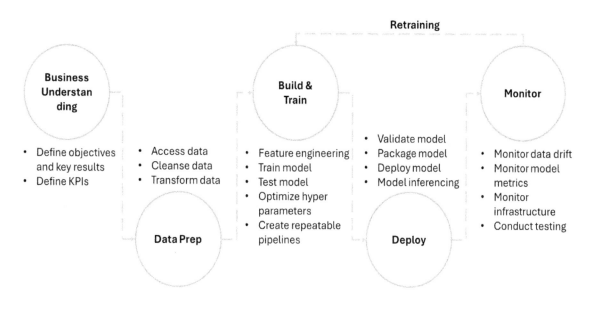

MLOps Flow

Use Of MLOps:

MLOps is a useful approach for developing and enhancing the performance of AI and machine learning solutions. By maintaining continuous integration and deployment (CI/CD) practices with close supervision, validation, and governance of ML models, data engineers, and machine learning engineers can collaborate and accelerate model development and production by using an MLOps approach.

MLOps, or machine learning operations, is a set of practices for managing the machine learning (ML) lifecycle. It involves tasks such as:

- **Experiment tracking**: Keeping track of experiments and results to identify the best models
- **Model deployment**: Making models accessible to applications by deploying them to production
- **Model monitoring**: Detecting issues or performance degradation in models
- **Model retraining**: Improving model performance by retraining them with new data

MLOps aims to improve the quality of production ML, increase automation, and maintain compliance with business and regulatory requirements. It's inspired by DevOps and GitOps principles and seeks to integrate ML models into software development processes.

MLOps can help streamline the process of running data science models, which can be expensive and time-consuming. Before MLOps, managing the ML lifecycle was often slow and laborious, and data scientists, software engineers, and IT operations often worked in silos. MLOps can help to:

- Unify the release cycle for machine learning and software applications
- Enable automated testing of machine learning artifacts
- Reduce technical debt across machine learning models
- Ensure that machine learning models stay accurate and up to date

Why MLOps important?

It is difficult to commercialize machine learning. The machine learning life cycle includes many complicated structures like data ingestion, data preparation, model training, model optimization, model deployment, model tracking, and much more. It also necessitates cross-team collaboration and hand-offs, from Data Science to Data Engineering to Machine Learning Engineering. To keep all of these mechanisms synchronous as well as working in tandem, stringent operational rigor is required. MLOps refers to the machine learning lifecycle's experimentation, refinements, and continuous improvement.

MLOps different components:

- **Data Management:** Data management includes processing data acquisition, storage, and preprocessing data through specific technologies. Proper data management can ensure good quality and accessibility of data for the training of models.

- **Model Development and Training:** Models are developed through different machine learning algorithms, and then the developed models are trained using data. It includes proper frameworks and tools for model development.
- **Model Versioning:** Like code versioning in software development, this approach keeps different versions of models along with the related data sets, therefore facilitating the management of model changes and iterations.
- **Deployment:** It is the process of integrating a trained model into a production environment, where the latter can make predictions or take action based on new data.
- **Model Monitoring and Management**: After deployment, the models must be monitored occasionally for performance and accuracy. Model management updates the model in response to data or business needs changes.
- **Automation and Orchestration:** Automation in workflows and orchestration within the machine-learning pipeline is cardinal at scale. This implies automating processes in data preprocessing, model training, testing, and deployment.
- **Collaboration and Governance:** Mechanism to enable teaming across Data Scientists, Engineers, and Business stakeholders to collaborate in an AI project, with governance in place on ethical AI practice, security, and compliance.

This integration is the foundation of MLOps, where the teams generate, deploy, and manage their machine-learning models efficiently and effectively.

Key Benefits of MLOps

The organization gains several benefits from implementing MLOps within the flow of machine learning models. Some key benefits include

- **Time to Market:** MLOps has reduced the lifecycle of machine learning from the data preparation and model preparation stage to deploying it as a model. This reduces the time it takes to usher in production models.
- **Improved Model Quality and Performance**: The continuous workflow—integration, delivery, and monitoring—of models ensures models always perform optimally, delivering the most accurate results.
- **Collaboration:** MLOps improves collaboration that is part of the data scientists' tasks, of the developers and operational engineers to share goals and work together effectively.
- **Scalability**: MLOps' best practices and tools help scale machine learning operations so that effectively treating multiple models and big volumes of data becomes easy.
- **Reproducibility and Traceability**: MLOps enable versioning models and data, ensuring reproducible experiments and the traceability of changes through a clear history, thereby adding accountability and transparency.

- **Cost Efficiency:** It drives a dramatically reduced cost in performing operations surrounding projects in machine learning through automation of repetitive tasks and resource optimization.
- **Regulatory Compliance and Security:** MLOps allows governance and regulatory compliance due to the mechanisms that can be formed for auditing models, data privacy, and security measures.

MLOps is about applying engineering discipline to the development and deployment of machine learning models. It's about making the process more efficient, reliable, and scalable, so that organizations can effectively leverage the power of AI.

LLMOps

LLMOps, or Large Language Model Operations, is a specialized subset of MLOps that focuses on the unique challenges of managing and deploying large language models (LLMs) in production. While it shares many core principles with MLOps, LLMOps addresses the specific characteristics of LLMs, such as their massive size, complex training requirements, and sensitivity to data quality.

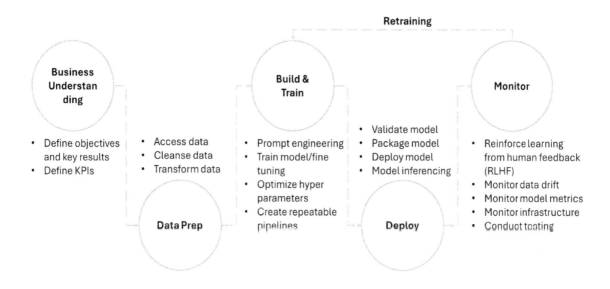

Retraining

Business Understanding
- Define objectives and key results
- Define KPIs

Data Prep
- Access data
- Cleanse data
- Transform data

Build & Train
- Prompt engineering
- Train model/fine tuning
- Optimize hyper parameters
- Create repeatable pipelines

Deploy
- Validate model
- Package model
- Deploy model
- Model inferencing

Monitor
- Reinforce learning from human feedback (RLHF)
- Monitor data drift
- Monitor model metrics
- Monitor infrastructure
- Conduct testing

LLMOps Flow

Breakdown of what makes LLMOps distinct:

Key Challenges and Considerations in LLMOps:

- **Computational Resources:** LLMs require significant computational resources for training, fine-tuning, and inference. LLMOps must address the efficient allocation and management of these resources, often involving specialized hardware like GPUs.
- **Data Management:** LLMs are trained on massive datasets of text and code. Managing and curating these datasets, ensuring data quality and addressing biases, is a critical aspect of LLMOps.
- **Model Size and Complexity:** The sheer size of LLMs makes them challenging to deploy and manage. Techniques like model compression, quantization, and efficient inference serving are crucial in LLMOps.

- **Prompt Engineering:** The performance of LLMs is highly dependent on the input prompts. LLMOps includes strategies for designing, managing, and optimizing prompts to achieve desired outputs.
- **Evaluation and Monitoring:** Evaluating the performance of LLMs is more nuanced than traditional ML models. Metrics like fluency, coherence, and factual accuracy are important, and human evaluation often plays a role. Monitoring LLMs in production involves tracking these metrics and detecting issues like hallucinations or biases.
- **Security and Privacy:** LLMs can be vulnerable to attacks like prompt injection or data poisoning. LLMOps must incorporate security best practices to protect against these threats and ensure data privacy.
- **Explainability and Bias:** Understanding why an LLM produces a particular output can be difficult. LLMOps aims to develop techniques for improving the explainability of LLMs and mitigating biases in their outputs.

Key Components of LLMOps:

- **Experiment Tracking and Management:** Tools and processes for tracking experiments, managing different model versions, and comparing their performance.
- **Prompt Engineering and Management:** Techniques for designing, storing, and optimizing prompts, including prompt versioning and testing.
- **Model Deployment and Serving:** Efficiently deploying LLMs for inference, including techniques for model optimization and scaling.

- **Monitoring and Evaluation:** Tracking key metrics, detecting issues, and evaluating the performance of LLMs in production.
- **Data Management and Governance:** Managing and curating large datasets, ensuring data quality, and addressing biases.

How LLMOps Extends MLOps:

While LLMOps builds upon the foundation of MLOps, it introduces specific considerations for LLMs:

- **Emphasis on prompt engineering and management.**
- **Focus on efficient inference and resource optimization for large models.**
- **Specialized evaluation metrics and monitoring techniques.**
- **Increased attention to security, privacy, and bias mitigation.**

By addressing these unique challenges, LLMOps enables organizations to effectively leverage the power of LLMs in a responsible and scalable manner.

CHAPTER 9
Building and Training Generative AI Models in the Cloud Infra

This chapter dives into the aspects of building and training Generative AI models within a cloud environment. It covers setting up the training environment, managing data, implementing distributed training strategies, and optimizing the training process for performance and cost-effectiveness.

Cloud Infra Foundation for Generative AI

Setting up Your Cloud Environment for Generative AI

This section guides you through the process of setting up a suitable cloud environment for developing and training Generative AI models. It covers key considerations for choosing a cloud provider, selecting appropriate compute resources, configuring storage and networking, and installing the necessary software and drivers.

1. **Preparing the Foundation**

   This section emphasizes the importance of a well-configured cloud environment for successful Generative AI projects. It outlines the key steps involved in setting up the environment.

2. **Choosing the Right Cloud Provider and Region**

   - **Key Factors to Consider:**
     - **Availability of Specialized Hardware:** Prioritize providers offering a wide range of GPUs (NVIDIA A100, V100, T4, etc.) and TPUs (Tensor Processing Units) suitable for deep learning workloads. Consider the specific needs of your models (e.g., memory requirements, interconnect bandwidth).
     - **Pricing:** Compare pricing models for compute instances, storage, and data transfer. Consider spot instances/preemptible VMs for cost savings on non-critical workloads.

- o **Regional Availability:** Choose a region geographically close to your data sources and users to minimize latency.
- o **Integration with Other Cloud Services:** Evaluate the provider's ecosystem and integration with other services you might need (e.g., data storage, data processing, monitoring).
- o **Managed AI/ML Services:** Assess the maturity and comprehensiveness of the provider's managed AI/ML services (e.g., SageMaker, Azure Machine Learning, Vertex AI), as these can significantly simplify the training and deployment process.
- **Popular Cloud Providers for Generative AI:**
  - o **Amazon Web Services (AWS):** Offers a wide selection of EC2 instances with GPUs and TPUs, along with managed services like SageMaker and Bedrock. Strong ecosystem and extensive documentation.
  - o **Microsoft Azure:** Provides VMs with NVIDIA GPUs and access to Azure Machine Learning and the Azure OpenAI Service. Strong enterprise features and integration with other Microsoft products.
  - o **Google Cloud Platform (GCP):** Offers VMs with NVIDIA GPUs and TPUs, along with Vertex AI. Strong focus on AI research and innovation.
- **Choosing the Right Region:**
  - o Consider data residency requirements and compliance regulations.
  - o Minimize latency by selecting a region geographically close to your data and users.

o Check for regional availability of specific instance types and services.

3. Selecting Compute Instances

- **Understanding Instance Families:**
  - **GPU Instances:** Designed for computationally intensive workloads like deep learning. Look for instances with high-performance GPUs and sufficient memory.
  - **TPU Instances:** Specialized hardware designed by Google for accelerated machine learning. Suitable for large-scale training of specific models.
  - **CPU Instances:** Generally not suitable for training large Generative AI models but can be used for smaller tasks or pre/post-processing.

- **Matching Instances to Model Requirements:**

  - **Model Size:** Larger models require more GPU memory. Choose instances with sufficient VRAM.
  - **Batch Size:** Larger batch sizes require more GPU memory.
  - **Training Speed:** More powerful GPUs lead to faster training times.
- **Memory (RAM) and Storage Considerations:**
  - Ensure sufficient system RAM for data loading and processing.
  - Use local SSDs for fast access to training data during training.
- **Example Instance Types:**

- **AWS:** p4d.24xlarge (A100 GPUs), p3.16xlarge (V100 GPUs), inf1 (Inferentia for inference)
- **Azure:** ND A100 v4-series, NV v3-series (V100 GPUs)
- **GCP:** A2 VMs (A100 GPUs), TPU v3/v4 Pods

4. **Configuring Storage and Networking**

- **Storage Solutions:**
    - **Object Storage (e.g., AWS S3, Azure Blob Storage, Google Cloud Storage):** Cost-effective for storing large datasets and model checkpoints. Suitable for data that doesn't require frequent random access.
    - **Block Storage (e.g., AWS EBS, Azure Disks, Google Persistent Disk):** Provides high-performance block storage for VMs. Suitable for storing operating systems and frequently accessed data.
    - **File Storage (e.g., AWS EFS, Azure Files, Google Cloud Filestore):** Provides shared file systems that can be accessed by multiple instances. Useful for collaborative work and sharing data between instances.

- **Networking Configuration:**

    - **Virtual Private Cloud (VPC):** Create a secure and isolated network environment for your resources.

- o **Subnets:** Divide your VPC into subnets for better organization and security.
- o **Security Groups/Network Security Groups:** Control network traffic to and from your instances.
- o **High-Bandwidth Network Connections:** Essential for distributed training to minimize communication overhead.
- o **Placement Groups/Proximity Placement Groups:** Place instances close together to reduce latency for distributed training.

5. **Installing Software and Drivers**
- **Operating System:** Choose a Linux distribution suitable for deep learning (e.g., Ubuntu, CentOS).
- **NVIDIA Drivers and CUDA:** Install the appropriate NVIDIA drivers and CUDA toolkit for your GPUs.
- **Deep Learning Frameworks:** Install TensorFlow, PyTorch, JAX, or other frameworks you plan to use.
- **Other Libraries and Tools:** Install necessary libraries for data processing (e.g., NumPy, Pandas), visualization (e.g., Matplotlib, TensorBoard), and other tasks.
- **Using Pre-configured Images/Containers:**
  - o **Deep Learning AMIs (AWS), Deep Learning VM Images (GCP), Data Science Virtual Machines (Azure):** Pre-configured images with all the necessary software and drivers installed. This greatly simplifies the setup process.

o **Containers (Docker):** Package your environment and dependencies into containers for consistent and reproducible deployments. Use container orchestration tools like Kubernetes for managing containerized workloads.

6. Security Best Practices

- **Access Control and Authentication:** Use strong passwords, multi-factor authentication, and role-based access control to restrict access to your cloud resources.
- **Network Security:** Configure security groups and network access controls to limit network traffic.
- **Data Encryption:** Encrypt data at rest and in transit.
- **Regular Security Updates:** Keep your operating system and software up to date with the latest security patches.

This section provides a comprehensive guide to setting up a cloud environment for Generative AI. By following these steps, you can create a robust and scalable infrastructure that meets the demanding requirements of training and deploying these powerful models. This solid foundation will enable you to focus on the core aspects of model development and experimentation.

Data Management for Generative AI

This section guild you on the critical role of data management in Generative AI projects. It covers the essential processes of acquiring, storing, processing, and governing the large datasets required for training and evaluating these models.

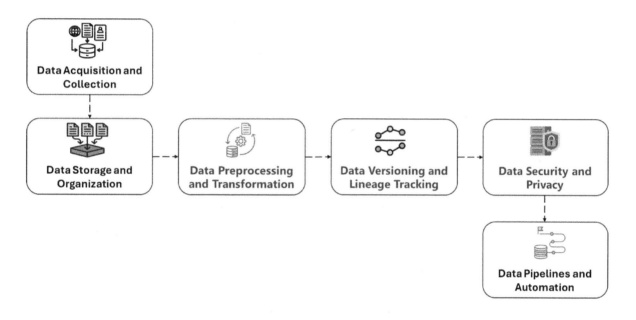

Data Management process flow for Generative AI

1. Fuel for Generative AI

This section emphasizes the importance of high-quality data for training effective Generative AI models. It highlights the unique data challenges and considerations specific to this field.

- Data Acquisition and Collection
- Data Storage and Organization
- Data Preprocessing and Transformation
- Data Versioning and Lineage Tracking
- Data Security and Privacy
- Data Pipelines and Automation

2. Data Acquisition and Collection

Generative AI data acquisition and collection refers to the process of gathering large amounts of diverse data from various sources, like text, images, audio, and code, to train generative AI models, which then use this data to generate new content that resembles the patterns learned from the training data; this often involves scraping publicly available information, utilizing APIs, and sometimes collecting user-generated data, all while adhering to privacy regulations and ethical considerations.

- **Identifying Data Sources:**
  - **Public Datasets:** Explore publicly available datasets suitable for your specific Generative AI task (e.g., ImageNet, LAION, Common Crawl).
  - **Internal Data:** Leverage existing data within your organization, ensuring proper data governance and privacy compliance.
  - **Web Scraping:** Collect data from websites, respecting terms of service and robots.txt.
  - **Synthetic Data Generation:** Generate synthetic data to augment existing datasets or address data scarcity issues.

- **Data Collection Strategies:**
  - **Data Pipelines:** Design efficient data pipelines for collecting and ingesting data from various sources.
  - **APIs and Webhooks:** Use APIs and webhooks for real-time data collection.
  - **Data Crawling and Scraping Tools:** Utilize specialized tools for web scraping and data extraction.
- **Data Licensing and Legal Considerations:**
  - Understand the licensing terms of public datasets and ensure compliance.
  - Obtain necessary permissions for using internal data.
  - Respect copyright and intellectual property rights when collecting data from the web.
  - Adhere to data privacy regulations (e.g., GDPR, CCPA).

3. Data Storage and Organization

Data storage and organization in generative AI guide you to the process of managing and storing large volumes of diverse data used to train generative AI models, which are designed to create new data like text, images, or audio, by identifying patterns within the training data and generating similar outputs; essentially, it's the infrastructure needed to hold and access the massive datasets required to power generative AI systems effectively

- **Cloud Storage Solutions:**

- **Object Storage (e.g., AWS S3, Azure Blob Storage, Google Cloud Storage):** Highly scalable and cost-effective for storing large datasets.
- **File Storage (e.g., AWS EFS, Azure Files, Google Cloud Filestore):** Suitable for storing data that requires file system semantics and shared access.
- **Databases (e.g., cloud-managed SQL and NoSQL databases):** Useful for structured data and metadata management.
- **Data Organization and Metadata Management:**
  - Establish a clear data organization structure to facilitate data discovery and access.
  - Use metadata to describe data characteristics, provenance, and usage.
  - Implement data catalog tools for metadata management and data governance.

4. Data Preprocessing and Transformation

Data preprocessing and transformation for generative AI involves cleaning, structuring, and converting raw data into a format suitable for training generative models, typically including steps like handling missing values, outlier detection, normalization, text cleaning, and data augmentation to ensure the model learns from diverse and high-quality information.

- **Data Cleaning:**
  - Handling missing values, outliers, and inconsistencies.

- o Removing duplicates and irrelevant data.
- **Data Transformation:**
  - o Resizing, cropping, and normalizing images.
  - o Tokenizing and cleaning text data.
  - o Converting audio and video data into suitable formats.
- **Data Augmentation:**
  - o Generating synthetic data by applying transformations to existing data (e.g., rotating, flipping, and adding noise to images).
  - o Increasing the size and diversity of the training dataset.
- **Data Splitting:**
  - o Splitting the data into training, validation, and test sets to evaluate model performance and prevent overfitting.
- **Using Cloud-Based Data Processing Tools:**
  - o Leverage managed data processing services for large-scale data transformation and preprocessing (e.g., AWS Glue, Azure Data Factory, Google Cloud Dataflow).

5. Data Versioning and Lineage Tracking

Data versioning and lineage tracking in the context of generative AI refers to the practice of meticulously recording changes made to datasets over time, as well as tracking the flow of data through the entire generative AI pipeline, ensuring transparency, reproducibility, and the ability to trace back the origin of any generated output to its source data and processing steps.

- **Versioning Data and Models:**

- o Track changes to data and models to ensure reproducibility of experiments.
- o Use version control systems (e.g., Git) for code and data versioning tools for datasets.
- **Data Lineage Tracking:**
  - o Track the origin and transformation history of data to understand data provenance and identify potential issues.
  - o Utilize data lineage tools and techniques.

6. Data Security and Privacy

Data security and privacy for generative AI involves practices to protect sensitive information used to train AI models, as well as user input data, by minimizing data collection, anonymizing where possible, implementing strong encryption, and ensuring proper access controls to prevent unauthorized data leaks or misuse, all while considering ethical implications and user privacy concerns.

- **Data Encryption:**
  - o Encrypt data at rest and in transit to protect sensitive information.
- **Access Control and Authentication:**
  - o Implement strict access control policies to restrict access to data.
  - o Use strong authentication mechanisms.
- **Data Masking and Anonymization:**
  - o Mask or anonymize sensitive data to protect privacy.
- **Compliance with Data Privacy Regulations:**
  - o Adhere to relevant data privacy regulations (e.g., GDPR, CCPA).

7. Data Pipelines and Automation

A data pipeline and automation for generative AI refers to a system of automated steps that efficiently move and process data from various sources, transforming it into a format suitable for training and utilizing generative AI models, essentially streamlining the data flow to ensure high-quality input for generating new content like text, images, or code, while minimizing manual intervention

- **Building Data Pipelines:**
  - Create automated data pipelines for efficient data ingestion, preprocessing, and storage.
  - Use workflow orchestration tools (e.g., Apache Airflow, AWS Step Functions, Azure Logic Apps) to manage data pipelines.
- **Automating Data Management Tasks:**
  - Automate repetitive data management tasks to improve efficiency and reduce errors.

8. Best Practices for Data Management in Generative AI

Best practices for data management in Generative AI include: establishing a strong data governance framework, prioritizing data quality, ensuring data privacy and security, implementing robust data labeling practices, carefully managing data access controls, and regularly monitoring data for bias and potential issues; all while considering the ethical implications of using AI technology and complying with relevant regulations.

- **Data Quality is Paramount:** Emphasize the importance of high-quality data for training effective models.
- **Data Governance and Compliance:** Implement robust data governance policies and ensure compliance with relevant regulations.
- **Efficient Data Pipelines:** Design efficient and scalable data pipelines for handling large datasets.
- **Metadata Management:** Implement effective metadata management practices for data discovery and understanding.

This section summarizes the key takeaways and reiterates the crucial role of data management in Generative AI projects. It encourages readers to prioritize data quality, security, and governance to build robust and effective Generative AI applications. By effectively managing data, you lay the groundwork for successful training, deployment, and ultimately, the impact of your Generative AI models.

Training Generative AI Models in the Cloud

This section focuses on the practical aspects of training Generative AI models within a cloud environment. It covers setting up the training environment, managing data for training, implementing distributed training strategies, and optimizing the training process for performance and cost-effectiveness.

1. Orchestrating the Training Process

This section emphasizes the importance of a well-structured training process for achieving optimal results with Generative AI models, specifically within the cloud context. It outlines the key topics covered in the section.

2. Setting Up the Cloud Training Environment (Recap and Refinement)

This section briefly recaps the key points from the previous chapter on setting up the environment, focusing on aspects directly relevant to training:

- **Choosing the Right Instance Type:** Emphasize matching instance type to model size, batch size, and training speed requirements. Briefly discuss spot instances/preemptible VMs for cost optimization.
- **Storage and Networking for Training:** Highlight the importance of high-performance storage (e.g., local SSDs or high-throughput network file systems) and low-latency networking for efficient data access during training.
- **Containerization (Docker) and Orchestration (Kubernetes):** Briefly introduce the benefits of using containers for consistent and reproducible training environments, and Kubernetes for managing containerized training jobs at scale.

3. Data Management for Training (Recap and Focus)

Data management for training generative AI involves collecting, cleaning, organizing, and structuring large volumes of high-quality data to ensure the AI model can learn accurate patterns and generate relevant outputs, while adhering to ethical considerations like privacy and bias mitigation;

key aspects include data collection, cleansing, governance, quality management, and ensuring the data is accessible for training purposes

This section focuses on data management aspects directly related to the training process:

- **Efficient Data Loading and Preprocessing:** Discuss techniques for optimizing data loading and preprocessing to minimize bottlenecks during training. Examples include using efficient data loaders (e.g., TensorFlow's tf.data.Dataset, PyTorch's DataLoader) and performing preprocessing operations in parallel.
- **Data Sharding and Distribution:** Explain how to shard and distribute data across multiple devices for distributed training.

4. Implementing Distributed Training

Implementing distributed training for generative AI involves splitting a large training dataset across multiple computing nodes (like GPUs) and coordinating the training process so each node simultaneously updates a shared model, allowing for faster and more scalable training of large generative models like GANs or VAEs, especially when dealing with massive datasets; key aspects include data parallelism, model parallelism, and using specialized communication libraries like NCCL to efficiently synchronize updates between nodes.

This section dives deep into distributed training strategies:

- **Data Parallelism:**

- o Explain the concept of replicating the model on multiple devices and distributing the data across them.
- o Discuss the advantages (simpler to implement) and disadvantages (communication overhead can become a bottleneck).
- o Provide examples of using data parallel training libraries (e.g., tf.distribute.Strategy, torch.nn.DataParallel, torch.distributed.launch).
- **Model Parallelism:**
  - o Explain the concept of partitioning the model itself across multiple devices.
  - o Discuss when model parallelism is necessary (e.g., for very large models that don't fit on a single device).
  - o Mention frameworks and libraries that support model parallelism (e.g., Megatron-LM, DeepSpeed).
- **Hybrid Parallelism:**
  - o Explain how to combine data and model parallelism for maximum scalability.
- **Managed Training Services for Distributed Training:**
  - o Show how to configure and run distributed training jobs using managed training services like Amazon SageMaker Training, Azure Machine Learning Training, and Vertex AI Training.
  - o Highlight the benefits of using these services for simplifying distributed training and managing infrastructure.

5. Optimizing the Training Process

To optimize the training process for generative AI, key strategies include: carefully curating high-quality training data, utilizing appropriate model architectures, implementing techniques like data augmentation and regularization, fine-tuning for specific tasks, monitoring training metrics closely, and leveraging advanced optimization algorithms to accelerate training while maintaining performance; all while considering the trade-off between model complexity and interpretability.

- Hyperparameter Tuning in the Cloud:
  - Discuss strategies for hyperparameter tuning in a cloud environment, considering the cost and time implications.
  - Explain how to use managed hyperparameter tuning services (e.g., Amazon SageMaker Automatic Model Tuning, Azure Machine Learning Hyperparameter Tuning, Vertex AI Hyperparameter Tuning).
- **Monitoring Training Progress in the Cloud:**
  - Show how to use cloud-based monitoring tools like TensorBoard, MLflow, and cloud provider-specific monitoring services to track training metrics, visualize training progress, and identify potential issues.
- **Checkpointing and Model Saving in the Cloud:**
  - Explain how to efficiently save and manage model checkpoints in cloud storage (e.g., S3, Blob Storage, Cloud Storage).
  - Discuss strategies for resuming training from checkpoints.
- **Cost Optimization Strategies for Training:**

- o **Spot Instances/Preemptible VMs:** Explain how to use these cost-effective instance types for fault-tolerant training jobs.
- o **Resource Utilization Optimization:** Discuss strategies for minimizing resource waste and maximizing utilization.
- o **Right-Sizing Instances:** Emphasize the importance of choosing the right instance type to avoid overspending.

6. **Training Specific Generative Models in the Cloud (Examples)**

This section provides concrete examples of training specific Generative AI models in the cloud. Choose 1-2 prominent examples and provide more detail:

- • **Example 1: Training a GAN for Image Generation on AWS SageMaker:**
  - o Briefly describe the GAN architecture (e.g., DCGAN).
  - o Show a simplified code snippet demonstrating the training loop using TensorFlow or PyTorch and SageMaker's training APIs.
  - o Highlight the SageMaker-specific configurations (e.g., instance type, distribution strategy, data input mode).
- • **Example 2: Training a Transformer for Text Generation on Google Vertex AI:**
  - o Briefly describe the Transformer architecture.
  - o Show a simplified code snippet demonstrating the training loop using TensorFlow or PyTorch and Vertex AI's training APIs.
  - o Highlight the Vertex AI-specific configurations (e.g., accelerator type, distributed training setup).

7. Best Practices and Troubleshooting

- **Performance Optimization Tips:**
  - Gradient accumulation for simulating larger batch sizes.
  - Mixed precision training (FP16).
  - XLA compilation (for TensorFlow).
- **Troubleshooting Common Issues in the Cloud:**
  - Network connectivity issues during distributed training.
  - Storage bottlenecks.
  - Instance preemption (for spot instances/preemptible VMs).

This section summarizes the key takeaways and emphasizes the importance of understanding the cloud-specific aspects of training Generative AI models. It encourages readers to experiment with different techniques and cloud services to find the best approach for their specific use cases.

Optimizing Model Performance for Generative AI in the Cloud

This section focuses on techniques to optimize the performance of Generative AI models, both during training and, crucially, for inference in cloud environments. Efficient inference is often the bottleneck in real-world deployments, so this chapter emphasizes strategies to address that.

- **Efficiency in Generative AI**

This section emphasizes the importance of optimizing model performance, not just for achieving better results but also for reducing costs and improving user experience in cloud deployments. It introduces the key areas of optimization covered in the chapter: model compression, efficient inference, and hardware acceleration.

- **Model Compression Techniques**

Model compression aims to reduce the size of the model without significantly sacrificing its performance. This leads to faster inference, lower memory footprint, and reduced storage requirements.

- **Quantization:**
  - Explain the concept of reducing the precision of model weights (e.g., from FP32 to FP16, INT8, or even lower).
  - Discuss different quantization techniques:
    - i) **Post-Training Quantization:** Applying quantization after training.
    - ii) **Quantization-Aware Training:** Training the model with simulated quantization to improve accuracy after quantization.
  - Highlight the trade-off between compression and accuracy.
- **Pruning:**
  - Explain the concept of removing less important connections (weights) from the model.
  - Discuss different pruning techniques:
    - i) **Weight Pruning:** Removing individual weights.

ii) **Filter Pruning:** Removing entire filters or channels in convolutional layers.

   o Highlight the benefits of combining pruning with fine-tuning.

- **Knowledge Distillation:**
   o Explain the concept of training a smaller "student" model to mimic the behavior of a larger "teacher" model.
   o Discuss the benefits of distilling knowledge from large pre-trained models.
   o Mention techniques for selecting appropriate training data for the student model.

- **Efficient Inference Methods**

Optimizing the inference process is crucial for deploying Generative AI models in real-world applications with acceptable latency and throughput.

- **Batching:**
   o Explain the concept of processing multiple inference requests simultaneously to improve throughput.
   o Discuss the impact of batch size on latency and memory usage.
- **Caching:**
   o Explain the concept of caching frequently accessed data or model outputs to reduce redundant computations.
   o Discuss different caching strategies (e.g., in-memory caching, distributed caching).
- **Model Serving Frameworks:**

- o Introduce popular model serving frameworks like TensorFlow Serving, TorchServe, and ONNX Runtime.
- o Discuss the benefits of using these frameworks for efficient model deployment and management.
- **Optimized Inference Libraries:**
  - o Mention optimized inference libraries like TensorRT (NVIDIA) and OpenVINO (Intel) that can significantly improve inference speed on specific hardware.

- **Hardware Acceleration for Inference**

Leveraging specialized hardware can significantly accelerate inference performance.

- GPUs:
  - o Discuss the benefits of using GPUs for parallel processing and accelerating deep learning computations.
  - o Mention different GPU architectures and their suitability for different workloads.
- TPUs:
  - o Explain the advantages of TPUs for specific types of models and workloads.
  - o Discuss the availability of TPUs in different cloud platforms.
- Specialized AI Accelerators:

- o Introduce other specialized AI accelerators like AWS Inferentia and Habana Gaudi.
- o Discuss their strengths and weaknesses compared to GPUs and TPUs.

- **Cloud-Specific Optimization Strategies**

This section focuses on optimization techniques specific to cloud deployments:

- **Choosing the Right Instance Type for Inference:**
  - o Emphasize the importance of selecting instances optimized for inference rather than training.
  - o Discuss different instance families designed for inference (e.g., AWS Inf1, Azure NVads A10 v5 series, Google Cloud T4 VMs).
- **Serverless Inference:**
  - o Explain the benefits of using serverless functions for deploying and scaling inference endpoints.
  - o Discuss the trade-offs between serverless and container-based deployments.
- **Edge Deployment for Inference:**
  - o Discuss the advantages of deploying models closer to the data source or users to reduce latency.
  - o Mention tools and services for edge deployment (e.g., AWS IoT Greengrass, Azure IoT Edge, Google Cloud IoT Edge).

- **Performance Benchmarking and Profiling**

- **Defining Performance Metrics:**
  - Discuss key metrics for evaluating inference performance, such as latency, throughput, and memory usage.
- **Using Profiling Tools:**
  - Introduce profiling tools that can help identify performance bottlenecks in the inference process.
- Benchmarking Different Optimization Techniques:
  - Emphasize the importance of benchmarking different optimization techniques to determine the best approach for a specific model and deployment environment.

- **Case Studies and Examples**

This section provides real-world examples of how organizations have optimized the performance of their Generative AI models in the cloud.

- **Example 1: Optimizing a Large Language Model for Real-Time Chat:** Discuss techniques used to reduce latency and improve throughput for a conversational AI application.
- **Example 2: Compressing an Image Generation Model for Edge Deployment:** Discuss techniques used to reduce the size and memory footprint of an image generation model for deployment on edge devices.

- **Best Practices and Troubleshooting**

- **Continuous Optimization:** Emphasize the importance of continuous monitoring and optimization of model performance in production.
- **Trade-offs between Performance and Accuracy:** Discuss the trade-offs between different optimization techniques and their impact on model accuracy.
- **Troubleshooting Performance Issues:** Provide tips for troubleshooting common performance issues in cloud deployments.

Delivering Efficient and Scalable Generative AI

This section summarizes the key takeaways and emphasizes the importance of optimizing model performance for successful Generative AI deployments in the cloud. It encourages readers to adopt a holistic approach, considering model compression, efficient inference methods, and hardware acceleration to achieve optimal results.

CHAPTER 10
Deploying and Managing Generative AI Models in the Cloud Infra

This chapter focuses on the practical aspects of deploying and managing trained Generative AI models within a cloud infrastructure. It covers various deployment strategies tailored for Generative AI, scaling techniques, monitoring, logging, and best practices for ensuring reliable, efficient, and cost-effective operation.

Operationalizing Generative AI

Operationalizing generative AI refers to the process of integrating AI models into production environments, ensuring they operate efficiently, reliably, and at scale. This chapter explores the key steps and best practices for successfully operationalizing generative AI models.

Key Steps for Operationalizing Generative AI

- Model Deployment
- Scalability and Performance Optimization
- Monitoring and Logging
- Model Management
- Security and Compliance

Deployment Strategies for Generative AI

Deploying Generative AI models requires careful consideration of various factors, including latency requirements, throughput needs, cost optimization, and the specific characteristics of the model and its intended use case. Here's a breakdown of common deployment strategies

1. Real-time Inference (Online Prediction/Serving)

This strategy focuses on providing immediate responses to individual requests. The model is deployed as a service that can process inputs and generate outputs on demand with minimal latency.

- **Use Cases:**

  - **Chatbots and conversational AI:** Generating responses in real-time during a conversation.
  - **Text completion and suggestion:** Providing instant text predictions as the user types.
  - **Image captioning and generation on demand:** Generating descriptions or images based on user input.
  - **Real-time style transfer and image editing:** Applying artistic styles or making edits to images in real-time.
  - **Music generation during gameplay or interactive experiences:** Generating music that adapts to user actions.

- **Infrastructure Considerations:**

  - **Low-latency network:** Crucial for minimizing the round-trip time between the client and the server.
  - **High-throughput instances:** Instances with powerful GPUs or specialized accelerators (like TPUs or Inferentia) for fast inference.
  - **Load balancing:** Distribute traffic across multiple instances to handle spikes in demand and ensure high availability.
  - **Autoscaling:** Automatically adjust the number of running instances based on real-time traffic patterns to optimize cost and performance.

- **Implementation:**

- **REST APIs:** The most common approach, using frameworks like Flask or FastAPI (Python) to create web services that expose the model's functionality.
- **gRPC services:** A high-performance RPC framework that can provide lower latency and better efficiency compared to REST, especially for complex data structures.
- **Serverless functions:** Deploying the model as a serverless function (like AWS Lambda, Azure Functions, or Google Cloud Functions) can be a cost-effective option for applications with infrequent or unpredictable traffic.

- **Challenges:**

  - **Latency constraints:** Meeting strict latency requirements can be challenging, especially for complex models.
  - **Cold starts (for serverless):** The initial invocation of a serverless function can experience higher latency due to the function's initialization.
  - **Cost optimization:** Balancing performance with cost can be complex, especially with autoscaling.

2. Batch Inference (Offline Generation/Processing)

This strategy involves processing large batches of input data offline and generating predictions or content in bulk. It prioritizes throughput over low latency.

- **Use Cases:**
  - **Synthetic data generation:** Creating large datasets of synthetic data for training other machine learning models.
  - **Generating marketing materials in bulk:** Creating numerous variations of ad copy, product descriptions, or social media posts.
  - **Generating large datasets of images or videos:** Creating training data for computer vision or video analysis models.
  - **Generating reports or summaries from large text corpora:** Processing large amounts of text data to extract key information or generate summaries.

- **Infrastructure Considerations:**

  - **High-throughput compute:** Optimize for processing large amounts of data quickly, potentially using distributed computing frameworks like Apache Spark or Hadoop.
  - **Cost-effective instances:** Spot instances or preemptible VMs can be suitable for batch workloads, as they are less sensitive to interruptions.
  - **Efficient data storage and access:** Optimize data access patterns for batch processing, using techniques like data partitioning and efficient file formats.

- **Implementation:**

- o **Batch prediction jobs on cloud compute instances:** Running scripts or applications that process data in batches on VMs or container instances.
- o **Serverless batch processing services:** Using cloud services designed for batch processing (like AWS Batch or Google Cloud Batch) to manage and execute batch jobs.

- **Challenges:**

- o **Throughput optimization:** Achieving high throughput can require careful optimization of data processing and model execution.
- o **Data management:** Managing large input and output datasets can be challenging.
- o **Scheduling and orchestration:** Managing complex batch workflows might require workflow orchestration tools.

3. Edge Deployment

This strategy involves deploying Generative AI models directly on edge devices, such as mobile phones, IoT devices, embedded systems, or edge servers.

- **Use Cases:**

- o **Real-time translation on mobile devices:** Providing instant translation without relying on network connectivity.

- **Localized image generation or style transfer:** Generating images or applying artistic styles directly on the user's device.
- **Enhancing AR/VR experiences:** Generating virtual objects or effects in real-time within AR/VR applications.
- **Offline functionality:** Enabling applications to function even without network connectivity.
- **Data privacy:** Processing sensitive data locally on the device to avoid transmitting it to the cloud.

- **Infrastructure Considerations:**

  - **Model optimization for resource-constrained devices:** Techniques like quantization, pruning, and knowledge distillation are crucial to reduce model size and computational requirements.
  - **Edge-specific hardware and software:** Utilizing specialized processors or hardware accelerators available on edge devices.
  - **Connectivity and data synchronization:** Mechanisms for model updates, data collection, and communication with the cloud (if needed).

- **Implementation:**

  - **Mobile SDKs:** Integrating models into mobile applications using platform-specific SDKs (like TensorFlow Lite or Core ML).
  - **Embedded systems libraries:** Using optimized libraries for running models on embedded devices.

- **Edge computing platforms:** Utilizing platforms like AWS IoT Greengrass, Azure IoT Edge, or Google Cloud IoT Edge to manage and deploy models on edge devices.

- **Challenges:**

  - **Resource constraints:** Limited computational power, memory, and storage on edge devices.
  - **Model optimization:** Achieving acceptable performance on resource-constrained devices can be challenging.
  - **Device heterogeneity:** Dealing with the diversity of hardware and software configurations on different devices.
  - **Model updates and management:** Managing and updating models deployed on a large number of edge devices.

Choosing the Right Strategy

The optimal deployment strategy depends on the specific requirements of the application:

- **Latency requirements:** Real-time inference for low-latency applications, batch inference for offline processing.
- **Throughput needs:** Batch inference for high-throughput requirements, real-time inference for handling individual requests.
- **Cost constraints:** Batch inference and serverless functions can be more cost-effective for certain workloads.

- **Data privacy concerns:** Edge deployment for processing sensitive data locally.
- **Connectivity:** Edge deployment for applications that need to function offline.

Understanding these different deployment strategies and their associated infrastructure considerations is crucial for successfully deploying and managing Generative AI models in the cloud.

Scaling and Managing Generative AI Deployments

This section focuses on the crucial aspects of scaling and managing Generative AI deployments in cloud environments. It covers techniques for handling varying workloads, ensuring high availability, monitoring performance, managing model versions, and implementing robust CI/CD pipelines.

Ensuring Reliability and Efficiency

This section emphasizes the importance of scalability and effective management for the long-term success of Generative AI applications in production. It outlines the key topics covered in the chapter.

1. Scaling Generative AI Deployments

Scaling strategies depend on the chosen deployment strategy (real-time, batch, or edge).

- **Scaling Real-time Inference:**
  - **Horizontal Scaling:** Adding more instances of the model serving service to handle increased traffic. This is the primary scaling method for real-time inference.
  - **Autoscaling based on Request Load:** Automatically adjusting the number of instances based on the number of incoming requests. This ensures that resources are allocated efficiently and costs are optimized.
  - **Autoscaling based on Resource Utilization:** Scaling based on CPU/GPU utilization, memory consumption, or other resource metrics.
  - **Load Balancing:** Distributing traffic across multiple instances to prevent overload and ensure high availability. Load balancers can be configured to use different algorithms (e.g., round-robin, least connections) to distribute traffic effectively.
- **Scaling Batch Inference:**
  - **Scaling Compute Resources:** Increasing the number of compute instances or the size of the instances used for batch processing.
  - **Distributed Processing Frameworks:** Using frameworks like Apache Spark or Hadoop to distribute batch workloads across a cluster of machines.
  - **Task Queues and Orchestration:** Using task queues (e.g., AWS SQS, Azure Queue Storage, Google Cloud Pub/Sub) and workflow orchestration tools (e.g., Apache Airflow, AWS Step

Functions, Azure Logic Apps) to manage and distribute batch tasks.

- **Scaling Edge Deployments:**
  - o **Model Optimization for Edge Devices:** Optimizing models for resource-constrained devices to improve performance and reduce memory footprint.
  - o **Federated Learning:** Training models collaboratively on multiple edge devices without sharing raw data.
  - o **Model Updates and Synchronization:** Implementing mechanisms for efficiently updating models on edge devices and synchronizing data between the edge and the cloud.

Next to managing generative ai deployments

2. Managing Generative AI Deployments

Effective management practices are crucial for maintaining the performance, reliability, and security of deployed models.

- **Model Versioning and Rollback:**
  - o Tracking different versions of models and providing the ability to roll back to previous versions if needed.
  - o Using model registries or artifact repositories to manage model versions.
- **Monitoring and Logging (with Generative AI Specifics):**
  - o **Standard Metrics:** Monitoring standard metrics like latency, throughput, error rates, and resource utilization.

- o **Generative AI Specific Metrics:** Monitoring the quality, diversity, and coherence of generated outputs. This can involve human evaluation or automated metrics (e.g., Inception Score, FID, BLEU/ROUGE).
- o **Monitoring for Bias and Toxicity:** Implementing methods to detect and mitigate bias and toxicity in generated content.
- o **Logging:** Collecting logs from the model serving service and other components of the deployment to troubleshoot issues and analyze performance.

- **Security and Access Control:**
  - o Implementing strong access control policies to restrict access to deployed models and data.
  - o Using authentication and authorization mechanisms to protect API endpoints.
  - o Regularly scanning for vulnerabilities and applying security patches.

- **Cost Management:**
  - o Optimizing resource utilization to minimize costs.
  - o Using cost-effective instance types and pricing models (e.g., spot instances, reserved instances).
  - o Monitoring cloud spending and implementing cost control measures.

Next is continuous Integration/Continuous Deployment (CI/CD) for Generative AI

3. Continuous Integration/Continuous Deployment (CI/CD) for Generative AI

Implementing CI/CD pipelines automates the process of building, testing, and deploying new model versions, ensuring faster iteration and improved reliability.

- **Building CI/CD Pipelines:**
    - Automating the model training process.
    - Automating model evaluation and testing.
    - Automating model deployment and rollback.
- **Integrating with Model Registries:**
    - Using model registries to store and manage model versions.
- **Automated Testing for Generative Models:**
    - Implementing automated tests to evaluate the quality and performance of generated outputs. This can be challenging for generative models and often involves a combination of automated metrics and human evaluation.

Next is Infrastructure as Code

4. Infrastructure as Code (IaC)

- Using IaC tools (e.g., Terraform, CloudFormation, Pulumi) to manage and provision cloud infrastructure. This enables infrastructure to be treated as code, allowing for version control, automation, and reproducibility.

Next is Case Studies

5. Case Studies and Examples (Scaling and Management Focus)

This section should include real-world examples of how organizations are scaling and managing their Generative AI deployments in the cloud. Focus on different scaling strategies, monitoring techniques, and CI/CD implementations.

Next is understanding best practices

6. Best Practices for Scaling and Managing Generative AI Deployments
- **Start Small and Iterate:** Begin with a small-scale deployment and gradually scale up as needed.
- **Monitor Performance Closely:** Continuously monitor model performance and identify potential bottlenecks.
- **Automate as Much as Possible:** Automate scaling, deployment, and monitoring tasks to improve efficiency and reduce errors.
- **Implement Robust Security Measures:** Protect deployed models and data from unauthorized access and modification.

This section summarizes the key takeaways and emphasizes the importance of scalability and effective management for the long-term success of Generative AI applications. By implementing the strategies and best practices discussed in this section, organizations can ensure that their Generative AI deployments are reliable, efficient, and cost-effective.

Monitoring, Logging, and Observability for Generative AI in the Cloud

This section focuses on the critical aspects of monitoring, logging, and observability for deployed Generative AI models in cloud environments. Effective monitoring allows you to track performance, detect issues, and ensure the reliability and quality of your AI applications. Observability goes a step further, providing deeper insights into the internal workings of your system.

Maintaining Visibility and Control

This section emphasizes the importance of robust monitoring, logging, and observability practices for maintaining the health and performance of Generative AI deployments. It outlines the key topics covered in the section.

Key Concepts: Monitoring, Logging, and Observability

- Monitoring: The process of tracking key metrics and alerting on deviations from expected behavior. Focuses on what is happening.
- Logging: Recording events and data generated by the system for debugging and analysis. Provides detailed information about what happened.
- Observability: The ability to understand the internal state of a system based on its external outputs. Goes beyond monitoring and logging to provide insights into why something is happening. This involves using

tools that allow you to explore, query, and understand the system's behavior.

1. Monitoring Metrics for Generative AI

Monitoring for Generative AI is more nuanced than for traditional ML models.

- **Infrastructure Metrics:**
    - **CPU/GPU Utilization:** Track resource usage to identify bottlenecks and optimize resource allocation.
    - **Memory Usage:** Monitor memory consumption to prevent out-of-memory errors.
    - **Network Traffic:** Track network bandwidth usage to identify network bottlenecks.
    - **Latency and Throughput:** Measure the time it takes to process requests and the number of requests processed per unit of time.
- **Model Performance Metrics (Generative AI Specifics):**
    - **Output Quality:** This is highly dependent on the type of generative model.
        - **Images:** Inception Score (IS), Fréchet Inception Distance (FID), Structural Similarity Index (SSIM).
        - **Text:** BLEU, ROUGE, METEOR, BERTScore, and human evaluation for coherence, fluency, and relevance.
        - **Audio:** Signal-to-Noise Ratio (SNR), Mean Opinion Score (MOS).

- **Diversity:** Measures how varied the generated outputs are.
- **Coherence:** Measures the logical consistency and meaningfulness of generated outputs (especially relevant for text and multi-modal generation).
- **Bias and Toxicity:** Crucial for responsible AI. Use metrics and tools to detect and mitigate bias in generated content and identify potentially harmful or offensive outputs.

- **Application-Specific Metrics:**
  - Track metrics relevant to the specific application, such as user engagement, conversion rates, or error rates.

Next is logging strategies

2. Logging Strategies for Generative AI

Effective logging is essential for debugging and understanding model behavior.

- **Logging Model Inputs and Outputs:** Log the input data provided to the model and the generated outputs. This can be useful for debugging issues and analyzing model behavior.
- **Logging Model Internal State:** Log key internal states of the model during inference, such as activations or attention weights. This can provide insights into how the model is making decisions.
- **Structured Logging:** Use structured logging formats (e.g., JSON) to make logs easier to parse and analyze.

- o **Log Aggregation and Management:** Use log aggregation tools (e.g., Elasticsearch, Splunk) to collect and manage logs from multiple sources.

Next Observability Tools and Techniques

3. Observability Tools and Techniques

Observability goes beyond basic monitoring and logging to provide deep insights into system behavior.

- o **Tracing:** Track requests as they flow through the system to identify performance bottlenecks and dependencies. Distributed tracing is especially important for complex deployments.
- o **Metrics Dashboards:** Visualize key metrics in dashboards to monitor system health and performance.
- o **Alerting:** Configure alerts to notify you of critical events or deviations from expected behavior.
- o **Using Cloud-Native Observability Tools:** Leverage cloud provider-specific observability tools (e.g., AWS CloudWatch, Azure Monitor, Google Cloud Monitoring and Logging).

Next Monitoring Model Drift in Gen AI

4. Monitoring Model Drift in Generative AI

Model drift occurs when the distribution of input data changes over time, leading to a decline in model performance. Detecting drift is crucial for maintaining the quality of generated outputs.

- **Monitoring Input Data Distribution:** Track statistical properties of input data to detect changes in distribution.
- **Monitoring Model Output Distribution:** Compare the distribution of generated outputs over time to detect changes.
- **Using Drift Detection Algorithms:** Employ statistical methods like Kolmogorov-Smirnov test or Population Stability Index (PSI) to quantify drift.
- **Automated Retraining Triggers:** Configure automated retraining pipelines to trigger when drift is detected.

Next Implementing Monitoring and Observability in the Cloud

5. Implementing Monitoring and Observability in the Cloud
- **Using Managed Monitoring and Logging Services:** Leverage cloud provider-managed services for simplified monitoring and logging setup.
- **Integrating with Model Serving Frameworks:** Integrate monitoring and logging with your chosen model serving framework.
- **Building Custom Monitoring Solutions:** Develop custom monitoring solutions for specific needs or metrics.

6. **Best Practices for Monitoring, Logging, and Observability**
    - o **Define Clear Monitoring Goals:** Identify the key metrics and events that need to be monitored.
    - o **Implement Comprehensive Logging:** Log relevant information for debugging and analysis.
    - o **Use Observability Tools for Deeper Insights:** Leverage tracing, metrics dashboards, and alerting to understand system behavior.
    - o **Automate Monitoring and Alerting:** Automate monitoring tasks and configure alerts to notify you of critical events.
    - o **Continuously Iterate and Improve:** Regularly review your monitoring and observability strategy and make adjustments as needed.

This section summarizes the key takeaways and emphasizes the importance of robust monitoring, logging, and observability practices for ensuring the long-term success of Generative AI deployments. By implementing the strategies and best practices discussed in this section, you can maintain the reliability, performance, and quality of your Generative AI applications in the cloud.

CHAPTER 11
Cloud Managed Services for Generative AI

Cloud managed services for generative AI offer organizations comprehensive solutions to build, train, deploy, and maintain generative AI models without needing extensive in-house expertise and infrastructure. These services help streamline AI operations, reduce costs, and accelerate time to market.

Cloud managed services for generative AI encompass a range of offerings that cover the entire AI lifecycle, from data collection and preprocessing to model deployment and monitoring. These services are designed to simplify and enhance the generative AI development process.

Overview of Cloud Managed Services for Generative AI

Cloud managed services for generative AI" refers to cloud computing platforms that provide fully managed services for building and deploying generative AI applications, essentially taking care of the underlying infrastructure, maintenance, and scaling, allowing users to focus on developing their specific AI models and use cases without managing the complexities of hardware or software setup; major providers include Amazon Web Services (AWS), Microsoft Azure, and Google Cloud Platform (GCP), each offering various generative AI tools and services like pre-trained models, APIs, and development environments

Key points about cloud managed services for generative AI

- **Accessibility:**
  Users can access powerful generative AI capabilities without needing extensive expertise in machine learning or infrastructure management
- **Scalability:**
  Cloud platforms can automatically scale resources up or down to meet the demands of training and running large generative AI models.
- **Variety of models:**
  Different cloud providers offer a range of pre-trained generative AI models for various tasks like text generation, image creation, code generation, and more
- **Security and compliance:**

Cloud providers offer robust security features to protect sensitive data used in generative AI applications.

Types of Cloud Managed Services for Generative AI

Data Collection and Annotation Services:
These services handle the end-to-end data preparation process, including data collection, annotation, and validation, which are critical for training generative AI models.

Benefits:
- **Scalability**: Ability to handle large volumes of data efficiently.
- **Accuracy**: High-quality annotations ensure better model performance.
- **Time Savings**: Reduces the time and effort required for data preparation.

Model Development and Training Services
These services support the creation, training, and tuning of generative AI models. They provide the necessary tools and infrastructure to build and refine models.

Benefits:
- **Expertise**: Access to specialized knowledge in AI and machine learning.

- **Efficiency**: Accelerates the model development process.
- **Customization**: Tailored solutions to meet specific project requirements.

Deployment and Monitoring Services

These services manage the deployment of generative AI models into production and monitor their performance to ensure they operate efficiently and effectively.

Benefits:

- **Reliability**: Ensures smooth deployment and continuous monitoring.
- **Scalability**: Easily scales to handle varying workloads.
- **Performance Optimization**: Monitors model performance and makes necessary adjustments.

AI Security Services

These services focus on protecting generative AI models and data from potential security threats, ensuring compliance with regulatory requirements, and managing risks.

Benefits:

- **Protection**: Safeguards models and data against breaches and attacks.
- **Compliance**: Ensures adherence to industry standards and regulations.

- **Risk Management**: Identifies and mitigates potential security risks.

Integrated AI Platforms

These platforms provide end-to-end solutions that cover the entire AI lifecycle, from data preparation to model deployment and monitoring, offering a unified approach to managing AI projects.

Benefits:
- **Unified Solution**: Integrates all AI processes into a single platform.
- **Simplified Workflow**: Streamlines the generative AI development and deployment pipeline.
- **Collaboration**: Facilitates collaboration among team members and stakeholders.

Examples of cloud managed services for generative AI:
AWS:
- **Amazon Bedrock:** A fully managed service providing access to a variety of foundation models from different providers.
- **Amazon SageMaker:** A platform for building, training, and deploying machine learning models, including generative AI.

Microsoft Azure:
- **Azure AI:** Offers access to OpenAI models like GPT-3 and Dall-E for generating text and images.

- **Azure Cognitive Services:** A suite of AI services including text analytics, language understanding, and speech recognition.

Google Cloud Platform:
- **Vertex AI:** A platform for building and deploying machine learning models, including generative AI
- **Google AI Platform:** Access to Google's advanced AI models like LaMDA for natural language applications

In the next section we will review comparison of generative AI cloud serverless services offered by Amazon Web Services (AWS), Microsoft Azure, and Google Cloud Platform (GCP):

1. **Amazon Web Services (AWS)**
   Key Services:
   - **Amazon Bedrock:** A serverless platform for building, launching, and running applications using foundation models. It supports models like Titan, Claude, Jurassic-2, and Stable Diffusion.
   - **Amazon SageMaker:** A fully managed service for building, training, and deploying machine learning models. It includes tools like SageMaker JumpStart, SageMaker Pipelines, and SageMaker Studio.
   - **Amazon Q:** A conversational AI service for building chatbots and virtual assistants.

Features:

- o **Model Variety:** Supports a wide range of generative AI models.
- o **Integration:** Seamless integration with other AWS services.
- o **Customization:** Allows customization and fine-tuning of models.
- o **Security:** Offers enterprise-grade security features.

2. Microsoft Azure

Key Services:

- o **Azure OpenAI Service:** Provides access to models like GPT-3 and GPT-4, as well as Codex.
- o **Azure Machine Learning:** A fully managed service for building, training, and deploying machine learning models.
- o **Azure AI Search:** A cognitive search service for building intelligent search solutions.

Features:

- o **Direct Access:** Direct access to advanced models like GPT-4 and Codex.
- o **Integration:** Seamless integration with Microsoft products and services.
- o **Security:** Enterprise-grade security features.

- o **Model Explainability:** Tools for understanding and explaining model predictions.

3. **Google Cloud Platform (GCP)**
   Key Services:
   - o **Vertex AI:** A unified platform for building, training, and deploying AI models. It includes Vertex AI Pipelines, Vertex AI Workbench, and pre-trained models like PaLM 2 and Imagen2.
   - o **BigQuery:** A fully managed data warehouse for analyzing large datasets.

   Features:

   - o **Integration:** Integration with Google services and tools.
   - o **Pre-trained Models:** Access to pre-trained models for various tasks.
   - o **Jupyter-Based Notebooks:** Support for Jupyter-based notebooks for model development.
   - o **Scalability:** Scalable infrastructure for handling large datasets and complex models.

Each platform offers unique strengths and features, so the best choice depends on your specific needs and preferences.

In this section, we will take a high-level look at the various generative AI solutions offered by these three cloud platforms. Detailed articles about generative AI in each of these platforms would follow later. We will also discuss the LLMs each platform supports, their features, use case fitment, integration capabilities, pricing, and security considerations. This article assumes that you're familiar with generative AI and it terminology.

Cloud Serverless/Managed Generative AI Services

Generative AI primarily focused on creating new content, such as text, images, and code, by learning patterns from vast datasets. It uses models like Generative Pre-trained Transformer (GPT) and Generative Adversarial Networks (GANs), allowing for creative tasks like text generation or image creation. Traditional AI, on the other hand, focuses on specific tasks like classification, prediction, and decision-making, using supervised learning and models like decision trees or neural networks. While generative AI excels at open-ended and creative tasks, traditional AI is more analytical and used for optimization, prediction, and automation.

Our roundup of the top generative AI offerings from AWS, Azure, and Google Cloud.

Cloud platforms like Amazon **Web Services (AWS), Microsoft Azure, and Google** Cloud provide a variety of tools and services to make generative AI accessible to everyone. **Large Language Models (LLMs),** which are central to Generative AI, can generate human-like text, write code, create images, and perform various other tasks.

Cloud Platforms for Generative AI and LLMs

Functions	AWS	Azure	GCP
Primary Generative AI Service	Bedrock	Azure OpenAI Service	Vertex AI
	SageMaker		
Primary LLMs	AI21 Labs Jurassic2	OpenAI GPT3	PaLM 2
	Anthropic Claude	GPT4	Imagen
	Stability AI Stable Diffusion	Codex	Gemini
	Amazon Titan models		

Let's understand each service in detail and it's case studies

Amazon Web Services (AWS)

Amazon Bedrock:

Amazon Bedrock is a fully managed service that simplifies the process of building and scaling generative AI applications using foundation models. Amazon Bedrock provides access to multiple third-party foundation models from AI21 Labs, Anthropic, Stability AI, and Amazon's proprietary Titan models. This flexibility allows users to choose from different models depending on their specific needs.

Here are some key features and benefits:

- **Key Features:**
  - **Foundation Models:** Access to high-performing foundation models from leading AI companies like AI21 Labs, Anthropic, Cohere, Meta, Mistral AI, Stability AI, and Amazon.
  - **Unified API:** A single API to interact with different foundation models, making it easy to switch between models and upgrade to the latest versions with minimal code changes.
  - **Customization:** Privately customize foundation models with your data using techniques such as fine-tuning and Retrieval Augmented Generation (RAG).
  - **Serverless:** No need to manage infrastructure, as Bedrock is fully managed and serverless.
  - **Security and Privacy:** Built-in security and privacy features to ensure responsible AI usage.
  - **Marketplace:** Access to over 100 popular, emerging, and specialized foundation models through the Bedrock Marketplace.

- **Benefits:**
  - **Ease of Use:** Simplifies the process of experimenting with and evaluating top foundation models for your use case.
  - **Scalability:** Easily scale generative AI applications without managing infrastructure.
  - **Integration:** Seamlessly integrate generative AI capabilities into your applications using AWS services.

- o **Flexibility:** Choose from a wide range of foundation models to find the best fit for your application.

- **Use Cases:**
  - o **Text Generation:** Generate text for applications like chatbots, virtual assistants, and content creation.
  - o **Image Generation:** Create realistic images for use in various applications.
  - o **Summarization:** Summarize large documents or datasets.
  - o **Question Answering:** Build systems that can answer questions based on provided data.

- **Model Variety**
  Provides access to multiple LLMs from various providers, giving users flexibility based on their use cases.

- **Integration with AWS Services**
  Bedrock integrates seamlessly with AWS services like Lambda and SageMaker, allowing users to build, deploy, manage and access AI models efficiently.

Let's Understand How LLM FM Support AWS Bedrock

Supported LLMs:

- **Titan**

  Amazon Titan are a family of models built by AWS that are pre-trained on large datasets, which makes them powerful, general-purpose models. The Titan models are optimized for tasks such as summarization, text generation, search queries, and chatbot applications. These models are integrated into various AWS services, enabling seamless deployment across the AWS ecosystem.

- **Claude**

  Claude by Anthropic is designed with a focus on safety, providing outputs that are less likely to generate harmful or unsafe content. This makes it ideal for businesses requiring a higher standard of compliance and responsibility. This model is also highly suitable for building customer facing conversational interfaces.

- **Jurassic-2**

  Jurassic-2 by AI21 Labs is a versatile LLM with strong capabilities in text generation, content creation, summarization, and translation. It is designed to handle multi-language support with extensive control over outputs.

- **Jamba**

  The Jamba 1.5 Model Family by AI21 Labs has a 256K token effective context window, one of the largest on the market. Jamba 1.5 models focus on speed and efficiency, delivering up to 2.5x faster inference than leading models of comparable size. Jamba supports function calling/ tool use, structured output (JSON) and documents API.

- **Llama**

Llama 2 and Llama 3 family models are published by Meta. Llama 2 is a high-performance, auto-regressive language model designed for developers. It uses an optimized transformer architecture and pretrained models are trained on 2 trillion tokens with a 4k context length. Llama 3 is an accessible, open large language model (LLM) designed for developers, researchers, and businesses to build, experiment, and responsibly scale their generative AI ideas.

- **Stable Diffusion**
  Stable Diffusion by Stability AI is primarily used for image generation, and AWS provides comprehensive support for this model via Bedrock. It is ideal for creative projects involving art, design, and media.

Here's an example of how you can use **Amazon Bedrock** to build a generative AI application:

Building a Text Generation Application with Amazon Bedrock

Below are steps where you can build your own text generation application.

Step 1: Set Up Your Environment

1. **Create an AWS Account:** If you don't have one, sign up for an AWS account.

2. **Install AWS SDK:** Install the AWS SDK for your preferred programming language (e.g., Python, JavaScript).

Step 2: Configure Permissions

1. **IAM Role:** Create an IAM role with the necessary permissions to access Amazon Bedrock.
2. **Attach Policies:** Attach policies that grant access to Bedrock and other required services.

Step 3: Create a Bedrock Project

1. **Initialize Project:** Create a new project directory and initialize it with your preferred framework (e.g., Flask for Python).
2. **Install Dependencies:** Install necessary libraries and dependencies.

Step 4: Write the Code

Here's a simple example using Python and Flask:

```
from flask import Flask, request, jsonify
import boto3

app = Flask(__name__)
bedrock_client = boto3.client('bedrock')

@app.route('/generate_text', methods=['POST'])
def generate_text():
    data = request.json
```

```
    prompt = data.get('prompt')

    response = bedrock_client.generate_text(prompt=prompt)
    return jsonify(response)

if __name__ == '__main__':
    app.run(debug=True)
```

Step 5: Deploy the Application
1. **Containerize**: Containerize your application using Docker.
2. **Deploy**: Deploy the containerized application to a cloud service like AWS Elastic Container Service (ECS) or Kubernetes.

Step 6: Test the Application
1. **Send Requests**: Send POST requests to the /generate_text endpoint with different prompts to test the text generation capabilities.
2. **Monitor**: Monitor the application's performance and usage.

This example demonstrates how to set up a basic text generation application using Amazon Bedrock. You can expand on this by adding more features, such as integrating with other AWS services, implementing authentication, and improving error handling.

Azure Cloud

Azure OpenAI Service

Azure OpenAI Service is a powerful tool that allows you to build custom generative AI solutions using advanced AI models from OpenAI and other leading AI companies. Azure OpenAI Service provides access to OpenAI's suite of models, including GPT-4 and Codex, on the Microsoft Azure platform. Microsoft's partnership with OpenAI makes Azure one of the most prominent platforms for deploying generative AI applications, giving users access to some of the most powerful LLMs on the market.

Here are some key features and benefits:

Key Features:

- **Advanced Models:** Access to models like GPT-4, GPT-4o, GPT-4 Turbo with Vision, GPT-3.5-Turbo, and DALL-E 3.
- **REST API and SDKs:** Use REST APIs or SDKs (Python, JavaScript, etc.) to integrate AI capabilities into your applications.
- **Content Filtering:** Built-in content filtering to ensure responsible AI usage.
- **Responsible AI:** Commitment to responsible AI principles, including transparency, safety, and ethical use.

- **Integration:** Seamless integration with other Azure AI services like Azure Machine Learning, Azure AI Search, and GitHub Copilot.
- **Direct Access to GPT-4 and Codex**
  Azure provides immediate access to these models, allowing enterprises to leverage the power of OpenAI's state-of-the-art technology.
- **Seamless Integration with Microsoft Products**
  OpenAI's models can be embedded within Microsoft Teams, Power BI, Power Automate, and other services.
- **Enterprise-Grade Security**
  As part of Azure, the OpenAI models come with built-in security features, including compliance with regulations such as GDPR, HIPAA, and SOC 2.

Benefits:

- **Customization**: Tailor models to your specific business needs, whether it's for content generation, summarization, image understanding, or natural language to code translation.
- **Scalability:** Easily scale your AI applications to handle varying workloads.
- **Security:** Leverage Azure's enterprise-grade security features to protect your data and models.
- **Flexibility:** Choose from different pricing models (Standard, Provisioned, and Batch) to fit your budget and requirements.

Use Cases:

- **Customer Support:** Automate customer support tasks, summarize conversations, and provide real-time coaching for agents.
- **Content Generation:** Create personalized marketing content, automate product descriptions, and generate digital art.
- **Data Analysis:** Analyze proprietary data for smarter decision-making in finance, healthcare, and retail.
- **Workflow Automation:** Automate routine tasks to optimize operations and supply chains.
- **Accessibility:** Develop assistive solutions like real-time transcription to improve accessibility.

Let's Understand How LLM FM Support Azure

Supported LLMs:

- **GPT-3 and GPT-4:**

  GPT-3 and GPT-4 are some of the most widely recognized LLMs for text generation, question answering, summarization, and conversational agents. GPT-4, the latest iteration, offers improved performance and reasoning over GPT-3.

- **Codex**

  Codex is a specialized version of GPT, trained for generating code. It can understand and generate code in multiple programming languages, including Python, JavaScript, C#, and more. It powers

GitHub Copilot, a tool for code suggestions directly in IDEs like Visual Studio Code.

Let's walk through an example of how you can use Azure OpenAI Service to build a simple text generation application. This example will demonstrate how to integrate a GPT model from Azure OpenAI Service into a Python-based web application using Flask.

Building a Text Generation Application with Azure OpenAI Service

Step 1: Set Up Your Environment
1. **Create an Azure Account**: If you don't have one, sign up for an Azure account.
2. **Create an Azure OpenAI Service Resource**: Go to the Azure portal and create a new Azure OpenAI Service resource.

Step 2: Configure Permissions
1. **IAM Role**: Create a role with the necessary permissions to access Azure OpenAI Service.
2. **API Key**: Obtain the API key from the Azure OpenAI Service resource.

Step 3: Install Required Libraries
Install the necessary Python libraries:

```
pip install flask requests
```

Step 4: Write the Code

Here's a simple example using Python and Flask:

```python
from flask import Flask, request, jsonify
import requests


app = Flask(__name__)


# Replace with your Azure OpenAI Service endpoint and API key
api_endpoint = "https://<your-resource-
name>.openai.azure.com/v1/engines/text-davinci-003/completions"
api_key = "YOUR_API_KEY"


@app.route('/generate_text', methods=['POST'])
def generate_text():
    data = request.json
    prompt = data.get('prompt')

    headers = {
        "Content-Type": "application/json",
        "api-key": api_key
    }
    payload = {
```

```python
        "prompt": prompt,
        "max_tokens": 50
    }

    response = requests.post(api_endpoint, headers=headers,
json=payload)
    response_json = response.json()

    return jsonify(response_json)

if __name__ == '__main__':
    app.run(debug=True)
```

Step 5: Test the Application

1. **Run the Application**: Start the Flask application:

   ```
   python app.py
   ```

2. **Send Requests:** Use a tool like Postman or curl to send POST requests to the /generate_text endpoint with different prompts. Example curl command:
   ```
   curl -X POST http://127.0.0.1:5000/generate_text -H "Content-Type:
   application/json" -d '{"prompt": "Once upon a time"}'
   ```

Step 6: Deploy the Application

1. **Containerize**: Create a Dockerfile for your Flask application:

Below code will deploy Docker container

```
# Use an official Python runtime as a parent image
FROM python:3.8-slim

# Set the working directory
WORKDIR /app

# Copy the current directory contents into the container
COPY . /app

# Install any needed packages specified in requirements.txt
RUN pip install --no-cache-dir -r requirements.txt

# Make port 80 available to the world outside this container
EXPOSE 80

# Define environment variable
ENV NAME World

# Run app.py when the container launches
CMD ["python", "app.py"]
```

2. **Build and Run the Docker Image:**

```
docker build -t my-flask-app .
```

```
docker run -p 80:80 my-flask-app
```

3. **Deploy:** Deploy the containerized application to a cloud service like Azure Kubernetes Service (AKS) or Azure App Service.

   Step 7: Monitor and Scale
   1. **Monitor:** Use Azure Monitor to track the performance and usage of your application.
   2. **Scale:** Configure auto-scaling policies to handle varying workloads.

This example demonstrates how to set up a basic text generation application using Azure OpenAI Service. You can expand on this by adding more features, such as integrating with other Azure services, implementing authentication, and improving error handling.

Google Cloud Platform

Vertex AI

Vertex AI is Google Cloud's fully-managed, unified AI development platform designed to streamline the process of building and deploying generative AI models. Vertex AI is a fully-managed, unified AI development platform for building and using generative AI. Vertex AI provides a full suite of tools and services, making it possible to deploy and train both pre-built and custom models. Google leverages its own large language models like PaLM 2 and Imagen to power its generative AI solutions.

Here are some key features and benefits:

Key Features:

- **Unified Platform:** Combines data engineering, data science, and machine learning engineering workflows into a single platform.
- **Integration with Google Services :**Vertex AI models integrate deeply with Google services like Google Search, Google Workspace, and BigQuery, making it easy to embed generative AI into existing workflows.
- **Vertex AI Pipelines:** Vertex AI Pipelines allow businesses to automate the deployment and management of large-scale machine learning models, including LLMs.
- **Pre-trained LLMs:** Provides access to pre-trained models, including PaLM 2 for text generation and Imagen for image creation.
- **Gemini Models:** Access to Google's advanced multimodal models, including Gemini, which can understand and generate various types of content (text, images, video, code).
- **Model Garden:** Offers a wide variety of first-party, third-party, and open-source models for customization and deployment.
- **Vertex AI Studio:** A visual tool for building, training, and deploying AI models without writing code.

- **MLOps Tools:** Purpose-built tools for automating, standardizing, and managing machine learning projects throughout the development lifecycle.
- **Integration:** Seamless integration with Google Cloud services like BigQuery, Cloud Storage, and Dataproc.

Benefits:
- **Efficiency:** Accelerates the development process with unified data and AI tools.
- **Scalability:** Easily scale AI applications using Google Cloud's infrastructure.
- **Customization:** Customize models to fit specific use cases with various tuning options.
- **Security:** Leverage Google Cloud's enterprise-grade security features.
- **Collaboration:** Facilitates collaboration across teams with modular tools and integrated development environments.

Use Cases:
- **Text Generation:** Create personalized content, automate customer support responses, and generate digital art.
- **Image Understanding:** Extract text from images, convert image text to JSON, and generate answers about uploaded images.
- **Data Analysis:** Analyze large datasets for smarter decision-making in various industries.

- **Workflow Automation:** Automate routine tasks to optimize operations and supply chains.
- **Accessibility:** Develop assistive solutions like real-time transcription to improve accessibility.

Vertex AI Workbench:

Vertex AI Workbench is a Jupyter notebook-based development environment for the entire data science workflow, and is designed to simplify the development of AI models, combining data and AI workflows into a single environment.

Key Features:

- **Jupyter-Based Notebooks:**
  Provides a unified interface for building and testing AI models.
- **Integration with BigQuery:**
  Connects directly to Google's data warehouse for seamless data processing and analysis, allowing for LLM training on large datasets.
- **Pre-Configured Notebooks:**
  Provides pre-built environments for common use cases like text generation, translation, and data analysis.

Let's Understand How LLM FM Support Vertex AI

Supported LLMs:

PaLM 2

The second-generation Pathways Language Model (PaLM) is designed for a wide range of text generation tasks. PaLM 2 is optimized for high-level reasoning, making it suitable for applications like summarization, translation, coding, and conversational agents.

Imagen

Imagen is Google's generative AI model for image creation, similar to OpenAI's DALL-E. It is optimized for creating photorealistic images from textual descriptions.

Gemini

Gemini is Google's cutting-edge model for multi-modal tasks, integrating text, image, and speech processing capabilities. This model is designed for more advanced use cases where multiple types of data need to be processed simultaneously.

Let's walk through an example of how you can use **Vertex AI** on Google Cloud Platform to build a simple text generation application. This example will demonstrate how to integrate a language model from Vertex AI into a Python-based web application using Flask.

Building a Text Generation Application with Vertex AI

Step 1: Set Up Your Environment
1. **Create a Google Cloud Account**: If you don't have one, sign up for a Google Cloud account.

2. **Create a Vertex AI Project**: Go to the Google Cloud Console, create a new project, and enable the Vertex AI API.

Step 2: Configure Permissions

1. **Service Account**: Create a service account with the necessary permissions to access Vertex AI.
2. **API Key**: Obtain the API key from the Vertex AI service.

Step 3: Install Required Libraries

Install the necessary Python libraries:

```
pip install flask google-cloud-aiplatform
```

Step 4: Write the Code

Here's a simple example using Python and Flask:

```python
from flask import Flask, request, jsonify
from google.cloud import aiplatform

app = Flask(__name__)

# Replace with your Google Cloud project ID and location
project_id = "your-project-id"
location = "us-central1"
endpoint_id = "your-endpoint-id"
```

```python
client_options = {"api_endpoint": f"{location}-
aiplatform.googleapis.com"}

# Initialize the Vertex AI client
client =
aiplatform.gapic.PredictionServiceClient(client_options=client_options)

@app.route('/generate_text', methods=['POST'])
def generate_text():
    data = request.json
    prompt = data.get('prompt')

    # Set up the prediction request
    instances = [{"prompt": prompt}]
    parameters = {"maxOutputTokens": 50}
    response = client.predict(endpoint=endpoint_id, instances=instances,
parameters=parameters)

    # Extract the generated text from the response
    generated_text = response.predictions[0]['generated_text']

    return jsonify({"generated_text": generated_text})

if __name__ == '__main__':
    app.run(debug=True)
```

Step 5: Deploy the Application

1. **Create a Model Endpoint in Vertex AI**: Deploy your model to an endpoint in Vertex AI.

2. **Containerize**: Create a Dockerfile for your Flask application:

```
# Use an official Python runtime as a parent image
FROM python:3.8-slim
# Set the working directory
WORKDIR /app
# Copy the current directory contents into the container
COPY . /app
# Install any needed packages specified in requirements.txt
RUN pip install --no-cache-dir -r requirements.txt
# Make port 80 available to the world outside this container
EXPOSE 80
# Run app.py when the container launches
CMD ["python", "app.py"]
```

3. **Build and Run the Docker Image:**
```
docker build -t my-flask-app .
docker run -p 80:80 my-flask-app
```

4. **Deploy:** Deploy the containerized application to a cloud service like Google Kubernetes Engine (GKE) or Cloud Run.

Step 6: Test the Application

1. **Run the Application:** Start the Flask application:

```
python app.py
```

2. **Send Requests**: Use a tool like Postman or curl to send POST requests to the /generate_text endpoint with different prompts.

Example curl command:

```
curl -X POST http://127.0.0.1:5000/generate_text -H "Content-Type: application/json" -d '{"prompt": "Once upon a time"}'
```

Step 7: Monitor and Scale

3. **Monitor:** Use Google Cloud Monitoring to track the performance and usage of your application.

4. **Scale:** Configure auto-scaling policies to handle varying workloads.

This example demonstrates how to set up a basic text generation application using Vertex AI on Google Cloud Platform. You can expand on this by adding more features, such as integrating with other Google Cloud services, implementing authentication, and improving error handling.

Summary

Hope you enjoined your learning with this book "Cloud Infrastructure for generative AI The primary purpose of this book is to bridge the knowledge gap between generative AI and cloud infrastructure. While numerous resources focus individually on AI algorithms and cloud computing, there is a lack of integrated material that combines both areas. This book seeks to fulfill this gap by offering detailed insights, practical guidelines, and real-world examples that showcase how cloud infrastructure can be effectively utilized to develop, train, deploy, and scale generative AI models.

You can use this knowledge as your first step get into generative AI There three main Cloud Managed/Serverless Genrative AI services are currently mostly used while writing this book.

1. AWS **Bedrock**
2. Azure **Open AI**
3. Google **Vertex AI**

We will be coming with more hands-on and practices in the next book with Gent AI Examples and more development topics.

Happy Learning
Thank You & Good Luck